AF352280

Philosophy in the Age of Science and Capital

PHILOSOPHY IN THE AGE OF SCIENCE AND CAPITAL

GREGORY DALE ADAMSON

Continuum

The Tower Building, 11 York Road, London SE1 7NX
370 Lexington Avenue, New York, NY 10017–6503
www.continuumbooks.com

First published in 2002

British Library Cataloguing-in-Publication Data
A catalogue record for this book is available
from the British Library.

ISBN 0–8264–6031–3 (hardback)
0–8264–6032–1 (paperback)

Typeset by SetSystems Ltd, Saffron Walden, Essex
Printed and bound in Great Britain by
Bookcraft (Bath) Ltd, Midsomer Norton, Somerset

Contents

Introduction

From today's perspective, we can safely say that the history of the West is not without direction. Almost in tandem, science and capitalism have progressed to where they now dominate and structure virtually the whole of existence. Through advances in technology, agriculture and physics, etc., science has not only given us control over the material world, it has transformed material reality into an extension of our needs and actions. Steadily modifying all other modes of social existence, on the other hand, capital now almost completely determines the order and form of material life. Together, capitalism and science have transformed the environment into a machine for sustaining human existence.

In terms of technology, medicine, psychology and economics, the complexity of both life and our understanding of it have certainly increased. Computing, electronics, plastics and engineering have given us the ability to manipulate practically every aspect of the objective world to the shape of our needs. Similarly, the medical, cognitive and biological sciences now give an almost complete picture of the workings of the biological body and mind. Capital also has so enhanced our understanding and control of social order and the production process that the economy can be said to 'organize' itself.

On the one hand, capital's ongoing global expansion is unfolding in precisely the manner Marx foretold. As we are now witnessing, capitalism will continue to expand until it has captured the entire world as its market. On the other hand, on the political level, things appear to be the reverse of what Marx predicted. As time progresses, capitalism is not seen to be less but more natural; class conflict is not increasing but diminishing and political consciousness has given way to the spread of liberal values.

The fact that from within modern civilization the changing world is being increasingly accepted as natural is evidence enough that, contrary to what Marx believed, the current movement of things not only conditions but is conditioned by consciousness. Scientific advancement, for instance, is perfectly complementary to the needs of the capitalist production process. Likewise, technological development continues to provide the ideal infrastructure for the economic individual. With information technologies, computer automation and the general mechanization of the material environment, it appears that both science and capital are part of a wider movement or logic of change.

If the way we are going is in some way influenced by the structure of thought, then the growing assumption that the material environment is natural can only be expected. Furthermore, as liberal subjectivity spreads, it is becoming increasingly assumed that things have always been this way, even during what could be termed a time of global revolution. In this light, the greatest dangers today are not so much the changes we are undergoing but the fact we are becoming less aware that we are in fact changing at all or that it could ever be otherwise. With every new development integrated into daily life as soon as it appears, it has become generally assumed that change itself cannot be anything other than natural.

The more science and economics come to structure the material environment, the more they become synonymous with reason and order. Accordingly, and in keeping with the binary nature of language, any critique or opposition to the way of things is invariably categorized and dismissed as irrational and antagonistic. And since, as Marx pointed out, anything opposed to capitalism will only make it stronger, today's anti-capitalist and anti-globalization protests have become more symbolic of disorder than a threat to the establishment.

If we are to have any sense of where we are going and why, the first and most urgent task is to establish a position outside of science and capitalism. Having cornered itself in language, this is something contemporary philosophy has been incapable of achieving. In fact, unable even to distinguish itself from science, philosophy has turned into its understudy. With advances in computing, neuroscience and physics underpinning the philosophy of mind, traditional philosophy is now regarded as more of a form of mental exercise than a source of knowledge. Accordingly, the scientist has replaced the philosopher as the 'authority' on life's big questions.

The age of science and capital can in many ways be characterized by philosophy's progressive demise: beginning with the Kantian elevation of science over metaphysics, then the enclosure of thought in language and most recently its deconstruction. Today, other than a brand of cosmetics, philosophy simply means business principles – '40 hotels, one philosophy'.

The state of contemporary philosophy and thought is probably best betrayed by the connotations attached to the word 'metaphysics'. Since the advent of Western New Age spirituality in the 1960s, the term has become most often associated with such things as the healing powers of crystals or the effects of payote. This predominantly vacuous usage of the term has been paralleled by its being discredited in 'serious' or institutional philosophy. Since Russell's time at least, 'metaphysics' has been used almost exclusively pejoratively, with similar connotations to mysticism.

To understand where it is we are going, and what we are leaving behind, it is essential that we develop a position outside of 'physics'. If we approach Marx from another perspective, then current changes suggest where this metaphysical position may be situated. Although the revolutionary consciousness Marx predicted would accompany the spread of commodification has failed to appear, we are seeing the ongoing destruction of the 'cultural', 'creative' and 'aesthetic' values that he saw to be its cause. In the last few decades, capitalist production has taken over virtually all areas of art and culture, reducing the likes of film, literature and music to entertainment, and culture to its material form. In every category, 'sensibility' has fallen to the lowest common denominator, with mass production being the sole arbiter of commercial value. While our command and understanding of the objective world have undoubtedly progressed, intuitively, aesthetically or, for want of a better word, spiritually, one can only hope things cannot get much worse. Since the dawn of postmodernity, virtually every aesthetic and political movement has petered out and every living culture become threatened with dissolution.

Rather than otherworldly, the metaphysical indicates that aspect of existence which lies beyond the scope of representation and is irreducible to material form alone. The fact that the advance of science and capitalism occurs in tandem with the demise of art and culture suggests where the metaphysical is to be found. Metaphysics begins from the fact that our lives and the material world in which we are situated are absolutely continuous. The one thing we cannot deny is that our affective apprehension of ourselves and the world around us is as indivisible as life itself. It is this continuity which differentiates the cultural and the aesthetic from the objectivity of science and capital.

Around the turn of the nineteenth century, Henri Bergson developed the fact of continuity into a rigorous metaphysics and demonstrated, through introspection upon the continuity of thought, the existence of a creative logic incommensurate with the mechanics of reason. The fact that although immensely popular in his day Bergson has since been discredited only serves to vindicate his claim that reflective thought, or what he termed the intellect, is not so much a fixed structure as a logical tendency governing the evolution of humanity. Rather than a commentary on Bergson, what follows is an attempt to continue his project and reveal the 'nature' of science and capitalism. Following this, the logic of continuity is further investigated in relation to creative thought, the evolutionary process and the nature of cultural and aesthetic difference. This metaphysical account of change and production offers an extra dimension to Marx's critique. One which, in the end, has the potential to provide philosophy with the means to guide us in a more sustainable and productive direction.

CHAPTER 1

Science and Continuity

where the nature of logic parts from the logic of nature

The present age is defined, determined and dominated by science. As the motor behind developments in communications, transport, manufacturing, medicine, warfare, agriculture, engineering, entertainment, psychology, sexuality and nutrition, science continues to condition the shape of the human environment. Almost every aspect of daily existence – our clothing, diet, cosmetics, cleaning products, medications, the car, telephone, televison, computer and the buildings we live in – all owe their existence to scientific development. Today, there is barely an inch left on the globe or a moment remaining in our lives that is not in some way influenced by the achievements of modern science.

On the whole, scientific enquiry aims to increase our knowledge of the structure and mechanics of material reality. More than simply improving our understanding of the world, science is the means by which we elude the forces of nature and change. In every branch of science, 'progress' signifies the measure of our control over material existence. The greater our understanding of process, the greater our ability to predict and regulate the environment. Rather than being simply labour-saving, technology gives us direct control of the environment by making it conform to our actions. The more we know about the structure and composition of nature, the more we are able to manipulate material order and bring it in line with our own needs and expectations.

In all, the more science progresses, the more humanity and its environment become moulded to one another. With developments in transportation, manufacturing, agriculture and engineering the globe is being steadily transformed into a machine for sustaining human existence. Furthermore, directed towards enhancing the health and longevity of the body, advances in medicine, hygiene and nutrition are turning the human into a machine for living. In this sense, genetic modification is no different to any other scientific practice. Unveiling the DNA has simply created a new field of engineering where the properties of matter are adapted to serve human ends.

Scientific understanding can be said to have progressed throughout modernity. The sciences advance not simply through invention and discovery but by continually accumulating centuries of knowledge and innovation. The Internet, for instance, is not strictly speaking an entirely new product, for it brings together numerous existing technologies, such as the telephone and personal computer. It is now evident that as science progresses, material society becomes increasingly uniform. The one requirement of innovation, in this respect, is that any new discovery complements and enhances the ongoing mechanization and integration of the social environment. Scientific development, therefore, defines not only the present age of the West but, in turn, represents the benchmark of global development.

As all forms of practice or knowledge other than the scientific are constantly being displaced and overtaken, modernity renders primitive everything other to itself. In this regard, technology is not the sole mark of progress. For instance, despite the fact that many cultures conceal a broad understanding of diet in their customs and cuisines, only science is recognized as 'discovering' the nutritional properties of food. Isolated from sensibility and cultural practice, nutrition is perceived solely in the chemical composition of the foods we consume. Accordingly, 'diet' has itself become separated from taste, being governed now by the amount of fats, carbohydrates, proteins and vitamins contained in what one eats.

In recent years the sciences have branched into all areas of human thought. As a result, every aspect of existence now has some material explanation. By combining computing and neurology, for example, the cognitive sciences have reduced thought to the computational capacities of the brain's motor-neurons and synapses. This is equally the case with sensations, emotions and affectivity in general which have all been reduced to the effects of material causes. Science, in this respect, is not only shaping the structure of existence but is transforming both the manner in which life is enacted and the manner in which we apprehend change itself. While the likes of the Internet, television and high-speed transportation have certainly transformed the nature of life, our affective responses to change, such as depression, anxiety and unhappiness, are no longer thought of as statements about our present state of affairs but pathologies that we ought to, and should easily, put right. Now that we are able to treat the likes of depression just like any other physical ailment by adjusting the brain's chemistry, there seems little point in according value or meaning to what it is that our emotions and affects might be expressing in themselves.

In keeping with this, the sciences are also taking over the centre-stage of thought. Now that the answers to everything are believed to lie somewhere between the big bang and DNA, little is considered beyond the reach of scientific explanation. While material forms are assumed to be governed solely by empirically demonstrable physical qualities, the whole of 'creation' is said to derive from the unpredictable forces of chance. The rise of modern science, in this sense, is almost directly correlated with the declining authority of religion. There has been no greater challenge to Western theology than the theory of evolution which has undermined both the need for and the validity of the creation myth. Despite the fact that many continue to maintain some form of faith, religion serves more as an antidote to thought than a stimulus: terms such as 'God' and 'creation' remain useful bandaids to the unanswerable question of what comes before the big bang.

In recent decades the scientist has also replaced the philosopher and the artist as authorities on life. On the one hand, relatively modern disciplines, such as sociology and psychology, have progressively taken over the concerns and undermined the authority of the 'humanities'. On the other hand, it is the scientist, rather than the philosopher, poet or theologian, who is now called upon to answer life's 'big questions', debate the virtues and vices of genetic engineering and describe the nature of social change. Science is even making inroads into the artistic mind, finding pathologies (such as Monet's myopia) beneath all and any form of insight.

The more science conditions material existence, the more the scientific point of view, from where everything is seen to have some material cause and, therefore a reason, comes to reflect subjectivity in general. To be 'unaffected' has become as much a requirement of a 'good' life as it is of good science. The malcontent are more likely to seek therapy than express their misgivings through protest and resistance. Objectivity, in this respect, is not only a social imperative, it is a product of science itself. The new generation of antidepressants and tranquillizers have probably done more to quell disaffection in recent years than policing has ever done.

Although scientific development has clearly transformed the nature of existence, it could be said that the world has never been accepted as more 'natural'. Rather than 'future shock' technological development is seen by most to provide all the right tools for modern life. Scientific materialism, in this respect, acts as the perfect epistemologi cal counterpart to the social materialism of capital. We now find the sharemarket employed as an exemplar of the physics of chaos and the marketplace compared to the evolutionary process of 'natural selection'.

While obviously implicated in the expansion of capital, the simple fact that scientific investigation requires investment in the unknown demonstrates that science itself is an independent force of change. On the other hand, the 'naturalness' of either capitalist society or the science that shapes it are barely questioned. While some may be opposed to genetic engineering and global warming, there is little in the way of analysis or even understanding of genetic science and the nature of the late industrial world. Science is generally assumed to represent the world as it is, beyond the veil of social and cultural differences.

As a result of the ongoing process of mechanization occurring in all facets of existence as well as the spread of information technologies, material society is becoming increasingly integrated and uniform. Consequently, science and economics have become synonymous with common sense and reason. Any practices or forms of knowledge deviating from the order of modernity are not only left out of the social economy but are now seen to be outdated. Opposition to the effects of the current movement of change, be it globalization or scientific progress, is also being increasingly marginalized and dismissed as irrational and uneconomic. As the modern social order expands globally, we find that anything that does not fit in with the social economy tends to be marginalized and excluded.

It is becoming increasingly apparent that the more science governs our lives, the less we understand or interrogate science itself. To a large extent, this is reflected in the rapid and comprehensive demise of philosophy. In one sense, the downfall itself can be attributed to the success of science. Now capable of providing concrete models of the brain and its workings, the cognitive sciences have usurped philosophy as the recognized authority on matters pertaining to thought. On the other hand, on both sides of the continental and analytical divide, philosophy appears to have reached something of a dead end. Despite the fact that some believe truth to be illusive rather than illusory, the failure of the post-Kantian project to reduce thought to language has left philosophy without a foundation. In response to the many ethical dilemmas that have resulted from scientific research, philosophy as a whole has failed to bring clarity to the problems faced, let alone provide any adequate solutions. The interminable inconsistency of logic as much as the idealism of presence not only question the veracity of meaning but undermine the relevance of philosophy as a whole which, as we are now seeing, has become incapable of transcending the level of opinion. In keeping with the dichotomous nature of language, philosophy is only becoming ever divided into an increasing number of competing positions.

The increasing acceptance of the reality of scientific representation has been greatly aided by the fact that science works. In this light, the deconstructive assumption that science constructs narratives of a reality we will never know, as well as the ongoing debates over the nature of scientific truth only add to philosophy's discredit. While philosophy has yet to agree on the nature of reality, science continues to transform the world to such a degree that what it represents will very soon be our only reality. By remaining caught in the problems of truth and reality, philosophy continues to ignore the fact that science does not merely represent the world but also reconstructs it. If we are to have any sense of where we are going, therefore, it is essential that we find a position outside of science from which we can ascertain the 'nature' of science itself – for, if not entirely responsible for change, science represents what we are changing into.

THE CONTINUUM AND ME

If there is one incontrovertible fact underlying any scientific method it is that the determination of objective data presupposes the isolation of a discrete unit at a distinct period of time. While the idea of a discrete atom may have been undermined by quantum theory, 'atomism' remains both essential and intrinsic to scientific representation. All scientific procedures, from taking measurements to the units employed, necessitate the division of space and time and presuppose an atomistic picture of the real. This atomism can be either actual, as in genetics, implied, as in the separation of discrete 'states' or abstract, as in the real number continuum.

Science as a whole is founded on the discrete which, being necessary for determining objectivity, conditions both the scientific method and its image of the real. Despite the obsolescence of classical atomic theory, 'particles' remain the primary concern of theoretical physics. Most importantly, the representation of space, time and movement in general is predicated on the mathematical continuum. As a consequence, the Eleatic paradoxes continue to undermine the veracity of scientific representation, as determining data and representing process both require the division of movement and change. Although movement may appear to be reducible to a series of steps, the paradoxes reveal division itself to have no end. With modern science virtually beginning with the calculus, which requires taking division to its infinite limit, resolving the paradoxes of Zeno, or what is now referred to as the continuum problem, has been seen to hold the key to providing scientific representation with a consistent foundation.

In one sense, the Eleatic paradoxes distinguish the series of positions traversed by a moving body from the trajectory along which it appears to move. According to Kant, the paradoxes illustrate the distinction between phenomena and the abstract perceptual framework that contains them. In doing so, Kant was forced to contain human perception within a transcendental framework, thereby denying direct access to the 'thing in itself' and perpetuating the Eleatic distrust of representation. The emergence of non-Euclidean geometries eventually undermined the Kantian solution. With the ongoing success of mathematical physics, the onus was on philosophy to resolve the paradoxes and provide science with a foundation that would be as consistent as its success.

To a large extent what we now know as Analytical philosophy grew out of the desire to solve the continuum problem. First eliminating the idea of an intuitive or, in Frege's terms, 'psychologistic' continuum, the aim was then to provide a consistent logical description of mathematical continuity. Intially, much progress was made: Frege, for instance, developed a purely logical definition of number, while Cantor came up with a formal proof of the numerical 'size' of the continuum. Convinced a legitimate explanation had been found, Bertrand Russell believed the continuum problem solved, declaring that science and philosophy had entered a new age of certainty:

> The solution of the difficulties which formally surrounded the mathematical infinite is probably the greatest achievement of which our own age has to boast. Since the beginnings of Greek thought these difficulties have been known; in every age the finest intellects have vainly endeavoured to answer the apparently unanswerable questions that have been asked by Zeno the Eleatic. At last George Cantor has found the answer and has conquered for the intellect a new and vast province which had been given over to Chaos and old Night.(Russell 1918: 65)

In contrast to Russell's tenacity, the validity of the new mathematical continuum was to prove shortlived. Contradictions appeared within Cantor's set theory and a new set of paradoxes emerged which simply revived the form of the age-old aporia.

The fact that the Eleatic paradoxes refuse to be resolved has not hindered scientific development at all. Mathematics works regardless of whether the real number continuum is proved consistent or not. In this respect, despite failing to resolve the continuum problem, philosophy did make great inroads into describing the logical basis to mathematics and scientific representation. Most notably, in demonstrating the logical inconsistency within Cantor's set theory, Gödel and Turing, amongst others, revealed the existence of a common form to all algorithmic processes. Confirming the parallel between the algorithmic and thought processes, what is now known as the Turing Machine has not only become manifest in the computer, the increased speed of computer-processing has greatly enhanced the scope of scientific representation.

While the simple fact that science continues to advance confirms a correspondence between thought and objectivity, the gaps within the mathematical continuum suggest that representation may not give a complete picture of reality. Just as a computer appears more capable of processing thought rather than actually thinking, Turing and Gödel further revealed that the algorithm cannot account for its own creation. Instead, they argue, even formal logic and mathematical reasoning cannot escape the use of 'intuition'. Nevertheless, if anything exists beyond representation and reflective thought, it is by nature outside the realm of science. Since philosophy has cornered itself in logic and language, we are effectively left without any position from which to gauge the nature of science and where it is taking us.

Representing the objective world demands isolating either an image or a unit in space and time. As with Zeno's arrow, the determination of any objective data assumes that process can be stopped for an instant and that subject and object are, in Derrida's terminology, 'present' to one another. On one hand, the Eleatic paradoxes presuppose this simultaneity between subject and object. On the other hand, infinite divisibility reveals that this can never truly occur as each present is infinitely distant from the next. Despite this, mathematical continuity remains central to the pervading conception of time. As Bergson points out, the coexistence of subject and object in the same present is assumed not only in determination but in objective thought as well:

> The principle of identity is the absolute law of our consciousness: it asserts that what is thought is thought at the moment we think it: and what gives this principle its absolute necessity is that it does not bind the future to the present, but only the present to the present. (Bergson 1919: 207)

Although illusory, the coexistence of thought and its object constitutes the foundation of all 'intellectual' processes. Both Zeno and the arrow are assumed to coexist in the same present he determines its position, just as the data is assumed to be present to his mind when he describes the arrow's trajectory.

Within the paradoxes, and scientific representation in general, movement is represented solely by a set of discrete points, images or numbers. And when, for instance, number is used to calculate movement, the unit then acts as a representation of thought as much as of motion. Just as Zeno's paradoxes assume movement is composed of discrete steps, our reliance on language has led us to assume that thought itself is a step-by-step process.

Although we do carry out a limited number of objective and sequential intellectual operations, 'thought' itself, including our perception of ourselves and the world, is absolutely continuous. If there is one thing that no one can deny, it is that the continuity in which we live, think and act, is absolutely indivisible since no one has as yet lived a divisible life. Although the paradoxes of Zeno demonstrate that there can be no 'next' instant, the impossibility of the 'present' is only revealed through our actual apprehension of continuity itself.

Absent from the Eleatic paradoxes altogether, elided by the scientific point of view and generally ignored by philosophy, our affective apprehension of continuity has generally been considered illusory. The simple challenge to this assumption is, however, that if the continuum is wholly discrete then where does the illusion reside? In actuality, affectivity is inseparable from our own existence. Our affections are moulded with the continuity in which we perceive, think and act. Within this continuity, the manner in which we are affected by the world, and by our own thoughts and desires, constitutes our immediate response to the environment and the changes taking place around and within ourselves. However, as the continuity of affective awareness occupies the same point of view as abstract reason, it is incapable of being made an object of thought and has, for this reason, been considered irrelevant to thought. On the other hand, as the Eleatic paradoxes confirm, the indivisible continuity of our affective consciousness offers us a perspective outside of, and on, the purely objective point of view of science. And, as Bergson took pains to make clear, the immediacy of our conscious duration also has the potential to provide science with the metaphysics it lacks.

THE SUBSTANCE OF PHYSICS

Continuity was first encountered in modern science with the discovery of gravitational and electromagnetic fields. In *Matter and Memory* Bergson points out that the physics of fields compromises the classical model of an isolated atom. With the work of Kelvin and Faraday, he argues:

> We see force more and more materialized, the atom more and more idealized, the two terms converging toward a common limit and the universe thus recovering its continuity. We may still speak of atoms; the atom may retain its individuality for our mind which isolates it, but the solidity and the inertia of the atom dissolve into lines of force whose reciprocal solidarity brings back to us universal continuity. (Bergson 1991: 200)

While Bergson's reputation may have waned, twentieth-century science appears only to confirm his fundamental insight. General relativity, for instance, revealed gravitation to be a universal force, uniting all material bodies in space and time. When the significance of general relativity is combined with the cosmological implications of Einstein's equation, $E=Mc^2$, which undermines the distinction between matter and energy, the material universe is united into what is essentially a substantial continuum.

The idea that the universe is composed from the continuity of substance is not exclusive to Einstein. In the *Ethics*, Spinoza constructs a detailed account of the real as a substantial continuum. Not surprisingly, Einstein believed modern science corroborated Spinoza's metaphysical outline of substance. Both, for instance, concur that material reality is continuous rather than atomistic.

Although Einstein and Spinoza conceive material forms as deriving from changes in the size and distribution of modes of an essentially continuous substratum, they continue to adhere to the classical notion of time as unchanging. Changes within substance, in this sense, are believed to be deterministic and reversible, as material processes are governed by the eternal and invariable laws of physics. Substance itself is, from this perspective, hardly distinguishable from Plato's conception of time as the 'moving image of eternity'.

In recent times, findings in areas such as quantum mechanics and chaos theory have challenged the classical or determinist conception of physical reality. Similarly, the idea that physical processes are reversible, conflicts with the cosmological implications of the entropy law which, when taken to its ultimate conclusion, makes change irreversible and places the arrow of time in the heart of substance. Although relativity has revealed that there is no universal time-frame, the continuum must be seen to be irreversible if we are to respect the ramifications of the entropy law. This is the essence of Bergson's confrontation with relativist physics in *Duration and Simultaneity*, where he argues that irreversibility must apply to substance itself – a position indirectly supported by Ilya Prigogine in his recent *The End of Certainty*. Ignoring the controversy surrounding Bergson's supposed 'confrontation with Einstein', the clearest defence of *Duration and Simultaneity* is to be found in Paul Davies and John Gribbin's description of the image of time that emerges with the union of entropy and relativity:

> . . . when we refer to an 'arrow' of time, we should not think of the arrow flying through the void from past to future; rather, we should think of the arrow as like the compass needle, pointing the way to the future, even though it is not *moving* into the future. (Davies and Gribbin 1992: 128–9)

Not only time, but change itself, must be seen to pass in the same direction. For this reason, time can no longer be considered 'absolutely relative', for all changes must be said to have a 'sign' or direction. As Prigogine confirms, this in no way conflicts with the time-dilation that Einstein predicted and experiment has verified (Prigogine 1997: 169). In fact, the metaphysical implications of general relativity and quantum mechanics demand that change is brought into time itself.

If, as modern physics suggests, no material entity can be entirely isolated in space and time, then all changes must in some way be implicated in one another and any change must transform the continuity of substance to some infinitesimal degree. It is often argued that this 'wholism' implies that doing the dishes in Tonga must necessarily have an effect on things, not only in Europe and China but neighbouring galaxies to boot. This, of course, doesn't stand up to empirical evidence, but neither is it a necessary ramification of continuity. We don't expect to see ripples on the beach in Normandy if we throw a stone into the Thames because the waves dissipate in water. Accordingly, we can assume that material effects and forces decline entropically in space and time.

While the likes of relativity, entropy and quantum mechanics contradict the idea of material atomism, they also reveal continuity to be the limit of representation. The continuity of movement and change, as the paradoxes of Zeno demonstrate, cannot be isolated or objectified. Further to this, since all reflective intellectual processes are, as Turing revealed, also predicated on the juxtaposition of discrete elements, the continuity of change is precluded from being an object of thought. This does not mean that continuity cannot be apprehended *in* thought. Precisely as Bergson has argued, our immediate and affective apprehension of conscious existence provides the surest confirmation of the continuity that exists at the limits of representation.

The only way in which time's arrow acquires any sense is through the apprehension of our own continuity. Although it is practically *de rigueur* within contemporary theoretical physics to begin with the temporal nature of process, the fact that time is immanent enfolds thought itself within continuity, implicating affectivity in the apprehension of change. The intuition of time as the indivisible continuity of process is what Bergson defines as 'duration'. Duration signifies not only the limit of science but at the same time expresses the foundation of metaphysics. The collective limits of the scientific representation of the real delineate a substantial continuum to which we ourselves are immanent. Rather than the 'stream of consciousness' or simply 'lived time', the intuitive apprehension of our immanence to continuity, where the duration of thought and affectivity express the continuity immanent to all processes, arises at the limit of thought itself, revealing that in thought which can only be thought and that in affection which can only be felt.

In the metaphysical sense, duration is not in any way the end of the problem but the beginning. It constitutes the basis upon which all philosophical problems must be stated: the theory of mind, the relation between mind and body, nature versus nurture, questions of meaning, desire, identity and so on, must all be approached from the point of view of time and continuity. Most importantly, continuity not only offers a position from which to evaluate the object of science and the nature of scientific representation, it provides the means of avoiding opposition to science and the irreconcilable debate of whether science represents reality or not.

BETWEEN REALISM AND IDEALISM

The first and primary task of philosophy must be to distinguish itself from science so as to gain a perspective on the 'nature' of scientific thought and representation. Rather than debate whether the objective world is real or not, the first thing that needs to be done is to account for the fact that science works. In this respect, the simple fact that it is now possible to transpose DNA from a fish to a tomato and have it produce the same genetic effect, should be proof enough that whether what science represents exists or not is no longer a valid topic of discussion. Given the extraordinary fact of genetic transposability, it seems rather unlikely that it is we alone who construct the narratives of DNA and evolution. Considering how much we are able to anticipate, control and manipulate the movement of change, it is now as much irresponsible as it is pointless to question the *existence* of material order. There is no longer any reason to regard the world as phenomenal, as genetic modification is all the evidence we need to demonstrate that DNA exists as a 'thing in itself'.

Historically, establishing the foundations of scientific thought and representation has revolved around the dual problems of the status of reality and the influence of the subject. Following Kant's precise reduction of the object of classical science to the faculties of the transcendental subject, philosophy has been divided between the extremes of realism and idealism. Today, the debate between realism and the postmodern descendants of Kantianism has become so insular that both science and the real are nowhere to be found. Accordingly, if we are to escape this impasse and make any steps towards understanding the nature of either the objective world or the science that represents it, then, as Bergson suggests, we must first forget the 'disputes between philosophers' over whether the world we perceive is real or not (Bergson 1991: 10).

Bergson proposes that 'common sense' tells us that what we perceive is real: that objects exist in extension, colours correspond to various wavelengths of light, etc. As science has repeatedly demonstrated, not only the material world but its secondary qualities – colours, sounds, tastes, etc. – exist as and where we perceive them: in the material properties of the objects we perceive, their densities, chemical composition and the wavelengths of light and sound they reflect or emit. Despite the fact that much of science is said to conflict with appearances, it must be remembered that the greater part of scientific advancement has been due to the development of prosthetic tools which enhance the range of our own organs of perception. The images we perceive around us must be said to exist in the world rather than the mind.

Since material reality provides the material that is common to the senses, perception need not be said to be 'of' something. If what we perceive exists then, as Bergson points out, our perception must also be 'some part of the objects themselves; it is in them rather than they in it' (Bergson 1991: 228–9). Rather than assuming the brain constructs a separate image of reality, the images we perceive exist in extension, either emitting, absorbing or reflecting the light that affects the nervous system. The 'mechanics' of perception, in this sense, arise from the relations between what can equally be referred to as 'images', the retina, the optical nerve and the brain. From here the brain represents, as Spinoza would have it, the 'idea' of the image. That is, what we perceive exists where we perceive it, the brain presents nothing more than our 'awareness'.

Since what we perceive exists in extension, perception in itself does not need to be seen to 'add' anything to the real. The sole function of the perceptive faculties is to act as a frame, admitting that which is of interest while at the same time filtering out that which is not. Just as a thermometer 'perceives' only heat, perception admits a certain spectrum of light and has a particular range of focus for dimensions and speeds of movement and change.

First likening the acquisition of data to taking a 'snapshot' of process, Bergson then begins his analysis of perception by imagining it stopped in the instant an image is apprehended. Within this frozen moment the real is reduced to a static materiality where extension, including the brain perceiving it, is an aggregate of atomistic components and the subject is devoid of both affectivity and the continuity of 'living' memory. From this perspective, perception in itself, or what Bergson terms 'pure perception', emerges simply as the faculty for isolating images, differing in kind from the inextensive attributes of affectivity and memory.

Although 'pure perception' exists, as Bergson puts it, 'in theory rather than in fact', the taking of a 'snapshot' of process is presupposed by scientific analysis, both in terms of physical measurement and the units of calculation, revealing the scientific subject to be ontologically indistinguishable from the instruments it employs. Moreover, while perception in general can be said to be predicated on framing the real, in actuality the isolation of a discrete objective image in space and time constitutes an ideal which can never be attained. This is also the case with the determination of objective data, which although predicated on taking the equivalent of a snapshot of process always takes place within a certain duration.

The instant represents an ideal which measurement and recording approach but can never reach. Through number, units and language in general, however, the ideal is actualized and process is encountered as if it were frozen. Through the medium of language and numbering, not only the representation of the objective world but equally of thought assumes the form of pure perception and, as a consequence, elides the continuity within which change and the production of difference occurs. The idealism of the instant equally introduces necessity into nature, rendering all representations of process, in Spinoza's terms, *sub specie aeternitatis*.

Because representation is derived or abstracted from the real, number, units and equations of motion, etc. are, as Aristotle puts it, potential to the numbered. Determinism, in this sense, can be seen to actualize the ideal limits of process itself. From this perspective, Newtonian physics appears neither wholly illusory nor, as the more earnest advocates of 'postmodern' science would have it, 'wrong'. Classical science as a whole represents the limit of process itself, where systems tend toward linear causality and infinite repetition as the ideal form of stability. Moreover, non-linear dynamics and chaotic systems essentially remain deterministic as forms of representation and only present a closer approximation of the transformation of actuality. Since the idealism of the instant underlies any numerical representation of process, the causes and movements immanent to the continuity of process are more like what Bergson terms 'tendencies' than laws, and can never be known objectively in themselves.

SCIENCE AND ACTUALITY

Although perception allows access to the 'thing in itself', the apprehension of objectivity is not 'unconditional'. Aside from the parameters which limit perception to a particular band of the spectrum and certain dimensions and speeds, it is also conditioned by the structure of the perceptual framework. In contradistinction to Kant, who regarded space and time as forms imposed on sensation, Bergson reveals spatial distinction to be abstracted from the contours of material extension. Accordingly, rather than having any particular form, space admits of any number of degrees, with topological, fractal, Riemanian and Euclidean spaces being various perspectives carved out of substance. The empirical self, on the other hand, or what Bergson refers to as the 'duration wherein we see ourselves acting', is structured in relation to practice (Bergson 1991: 186). From this perspective the space underlying Euclidean geometry and Newtonian physics corresponds to the most efficient space of practice and is, as a consequence, reflected in our constructed environment.

To say that material reality exists as we perceive it is not to say we perceive the whole of reality. As Bergson has demonstrated, in order to distance ourselves from the objective world as well as perceive aspects of it, consciousness does not 'add' anything to the real, but subtracts that which is of no interest. Perception, in this regard, enables us to sense certain wavelengths of light and sound and types of chemical composition, while at the same time isolating particular images. Although the perceptive framework does not necessarily have a fixed and transcendental form, as Kant believed, perception still must be seen to give structure to the objective world. In terms of vision, this framework constitutes the space within which objects are distributed and we 'see ourselves acting'.

The space we perceive around us is not wholly constructed, but can also be said to have a degree of existence. Although the real is continuous, the distinct material objects we perceive represent various contractions or densities of substance. In distinguishing things from ourselves and from one another in space, perception takes the tendency towards discrete material form towards its limit. In sum, perception can be seen to actualize the material differences and spatial separation that exists potentially within the duration of substantial reality. As consciousness has arisen out of substance, the form and order we perceive, as well as the space within which they are contained, must be seen to be actualized *as* the form of reflective thought itself.

In actuality, even the most solid and stable of substances has a finite duration. As discrete objects are contractions of time and matter, no material entity can be completely isolated from the continuity of change. Representation, however, takes the tendency towards material form and spatial distinction to its ideal limit, isolating forms from one another and in time. Most notably, in language, the noun represents an ideal form of an object – a form assumed capable of reappearing in any space at any time. This is equally the case with movement and change. Be it in the cinema or a differential equation, change is represented by stringing together 'snapshots of passing reality' (Bergson 1983: 306). Accordingly, scientific representation is not unreal but *too* real, and not ideal but 'idealized', presenting the world *as if* it were completely actual. The only limitation of science is that it cannot escape being overly precise. Euclidean geometry and Newtonian physics, for instance, represent a world that is completely actualized and infinitely repeatable. Chaos theory, on the other hand, does not present the 'true' nature of process, only a closer approximation of the movement of change.

Although during the twentieth century science appears to draw closer to the real, at the same time it discovered that reality does not necessarily comply with appearances. In fact, experience comes to be considered a hindrance to understanding rather than the measure of validity. Somewhat ironically, instead of transcending experience, the greatest part of modern scientific development has followed from the construction of technologies that increase the range and scope of perception, in both the quantitative and qualitative senses, well beyond human potential. Most significantly, it was the emergence of increasingly accurate measuring, recording and detection devices that facilitated the incorporation of mathematics into all areas of science. From this perspective, science can be seen to increase our understanding of the real by extending the range and possibilities of perception. While the greater part of science may be beyond the range of human perception, the fact that science relies on instruments that effectively enhance the senses themselves means that the real emerges as both the object and arbiter of scientific experiment. The structure of actuality is the ultimate end of scientific endeavour, which gives science itself the appearance of an autonomous and purely speculative discipline.

On a different note, although the development of modern science has paralleled the growth of capital, the two have evolved in the manner of independent series rather than in concert. Scientific development, in this sense, is distinct from the modes of production which actualize it, the relation between the two being not direct but contingent: as in the space programme and non-stick frying pans. Overall, existence is steadily being moulded along the ontological lines of what science perceives as the real. Science provides the material for production and determines the nature of practice. The mould, on the other hand, is not science itself but, increasingly, capital. Instead of determining science, capital plays a selective role, integrating a multiplicity of singular scientific developments into its various modes of production.

Although science and capital are qualitatively distinct they are both predicated on quantitative difference, making the scientific image of the real the ideal correlate of capitalist production. Despite the fact that capitalist production is predicated on scientific development, the end of science is not profit and the end of capital is certainly not the understanding of material reality. This is equally the case with militarization or, more specifically, war, where as the Manhattan Project illustrates, the potential uncovered by physics was harnessed by scientists working not for science itself but the war machine. It is such movements, beyond science, that ultimately give direction to change and extend the influence of science into all sectors of society.

Even though scientific thought is 'neutral', aiming solely to increase our understanding of the objective world, it has the effect of determining or mediating our conception of reality. Science, in this sense, constitutes the ontological basis to practice and production, and conditions the form of both by determining the nature of their content. However, the real is represented by science not in its duration but as pure 'actuality'. Since determination is predicated on the negation of continuity and science as a whole is conditioned by the instantaneous, the real is stripped of the duration of movement and change as well as the continuity traversing and linking all processes.

The more science progresses, the more our ability to control material order increases. As reflective thought is predicated on the linguistic representation of both objectivity and thought, and as the framework of perception is structured in accordance with the objective world, the more material and mechanized existence becomes, the more it appears to conform to our expectations. Our ability to perceive the world objectively is what allows us to turn material order to our own ends. The capacity to determine our actions in a world we can predict and transform has given us the ability to escape the forces of change. The fact that in language material order appears completely actualized has created an ideal end of human development, where, completely materialized, the environment is perfectly synchronized with the structure of reflective thought.

Aside from environmental issues and the ethical problems surrounding both scientific and capitalist development, they are both grounded on an ideal ontology. Representation itself portrays a material world that is entirely actual and presupposes a wholly serial conception of time and process. From this perspective, all changes are said to derive from the rearrangement of discrete parts. Within this material world, order amounts to stability and recurrence, form and mechanism.

It is no surprise, therefore, that the more science progresses, the more material and mechanized our lives become. With the body also reduced to the sum of its parts, ageing has become a form of disease, the body something to be moulded to suit current fashion and health the mechanical functioning of the organs and brain. In making life more material and mechanized we are effectively taking the tendency towards material form and mechanical order closer and closer to its ideal limit.

REFLECTIVE CONSCIOUSNESS, SPACE AND NUMBER

Devoid of any particular structure, the empirical conscious self, or the reflective point of view, consists of the subjective unity of an objective multiplicity: it is by way of spatial distinction that the images we perceive are distinguished from one another while the unity of the self renders the perceptual field a given totality. This synthesis of the one and the many constitutes the condition of objectivity in general. The abstract unity of the empirical self is literally the frame that renders the objective world a totality, while at the same time distinguishing the subject from its object.

Although, as Kant has demonstrated, the empirical I is distinct from the 'I think', the 'objective' or multiple self is inseparable from the synthetic unity of the reflective point of view. In addition to perception, the spatial unity of the 'I' conditions the intellect and its contents, such as language, as well as the conception of space and time. In its denotative form, language derives from and is determined by the distinction between the one and the many. The origin of language is the unity of reflective thought, while the simplest denoting term is the number one. Since, in itself, one signifies the unity of a whole which is, in turn, divisible into an infinite sum of fractions, it is mimetic of the abstract form of the intellect. The one is also the simplest form of language or denotation. The basic properties of the one, in that it refers to any singular entity irrespective of its intrinsic difference and as an abstract class appears to exist for all time, underlie all modes of denotation, including scientific units. In itself the abstract unity of the intellect appears to exist outside of time and is the basis of both the instant and the eternal. The unity of the intellect, in this respect, renders all objective categories inherently Platonic – as well as being the origin of Platonism.

As representation and analysis are predicated on the isolation of discrete images or units, all objective processes are necessarily reduced to the sequential or a series of steps. This restriction is equally mirrored in the intellect which functions through the manipulation of discrete linguistic, symbolic or imagistic elements. As a thinking mechanism, the intellect corresponds with the form of the algorithm, being in this sense the equivalent of the Universal Turing Machine. Since the content of thought is, in this case, equivalent to bare actuality as it is devoid of the movement of change, the intellect is limited, in ontological terms, to what Bergson terms 'possibility'. Anything the objective mind computes will only be variation of the already existent. Accordingly, restricted to the discrete, scientific thought and, incidentally, artificial intelligence are equally constrained to the limitations of the possible.

The abstract and mathematical conceptions of time also originate in the intellect or the structure of reflective consciousness. The unity of thought gives rise to the idea of time as an abstract medium within which movement and change occur. Objectively, on the other hand, time is conceived as a discrete series of distinct numerical periods. As with number and space, time is considered to be infinitely divisible, the instant being the direct equivalent of the infinitesimal.

The abstract and mathematical conceptions of time are purely intellectual concepts, originating with the elision of affective continuity. With philosophical attempts to establish the consistency and reality of the mathematical continuum, the experience of affective duration is invariably seen as illusory, limited to the subject and a hindrance to the proper understanding of time. Within science, Einstein's infamous declaration that time itself does not exist continues to hold a prominent position. Stephen Hawking, being the prime example, holds that the only real time is imaginary. All such views are in part reactions against the temporality of being for, as in the case of Hawking, their earnestness equally expresses a profound naïvety. The absolute, indivisible continuity of duration constitutes the life of both the body and the mind; we cannot think outside of this continuity and we certainly cannot live 'without' it. The continuity of duration is manifest not in the abstract unity of the intellect but the affective, living self which is at once body and mind and immanent to the duration of the universe as a whole.

On the other hand, the fact that in science and philosophy it is practically a given that the continuity of time is equivalent to a mathematical series attests to the degree the intellect dominates thought as well as our current sensibilities. When setting the alarm clock, catching the train and getting to work on time, we live to mathematical time. It is this form of time, however, which exists solely in the mind for there is nothing outside the continuity of our action, expressed in the effort of getting out of bed, and the boredom of waiting for the train.

Continuity does not simply indicate the limit of scientific thought, but exposes a dimension of substance irreducible to representation. As with quantum mechanics, that which exists only in continuity must be seen to be complementary to matter. This is equally the case with the intellect, which is accompanied by a continuous domain of sense. In itself, however, the real is a process of modulation where the continuous is implicated in the variation of modes. This continuous duration is the movement in which change and the production of difference take place. Being irreducible to either the movement and distribution of elements, or an algorithmic series, the continuity of change is incommensurable to scientific thought. Rather than symbolizing the impossible, however, Bergson finds in continuity the logic of production and the grounds for an equally productive mode of thought.

NUMBER, LOGIC AND THEOLOGY

The primary obstacles to understanding the nature of scientific thought are the current trend towards scientific realism and the ongoing reluctance to acknowledge anything outside of logic and reason. Although scientific representation has been shown to be devoid of a wholly consistent foundation, the likes of intuition and metaphysics continue to be associated with mysticism. This attitude is prevalent not only within science but dominates Anglo-American philosophy.

The reluctance to acknowledge anything beyond the limits of logic and reason continues in the ongoing dismissal of Bergsonism. In Anglo-American philosophical history, Bergson's current status can be traced back to Bertrand Russell's paper, entitled 'The Philosophy of Bergson', delivered to the Cambridge 'Heretics' in 1912. This lecture, which not only drew a large audience but was published as an independent pamphlet, in *The Monist* and later in summary in Russell's *History of Western Philosophy*, had a great impact on Bergson's reputation, signalling the abrupt end to his immense popularity in Britain. As his biographer Alan Wood recounts, the lecture also marked the occasion of Russell's ascendance into philosophical notoriety:

> Bergson's mystical philosophy of evolution was then enjoying a tremendous vogue, which Russell set out to demolish; there was an eager audience to hear him, and everyone had a sense of a great occasion. The lecture can be found reprinted in Russell's *History of Western Philosophy*; to enjoy its savour, the reader must imagine it delivered in Russell's dry, precise and ironic voice, and punctuated by the laughter and applause which greeted his sallies. It was an event of some importance in Russell's life, helping to re-establish him as one of the leading figures in Cambridge; and especially because it was his first big success as a public speaker. (Wood 1957: 89)

Historically, this event is equally symbolic of a wider transformation in the history of Anglo-American thought. Russell's displacement of Bergsonism parallels the emergence of the analytic tradition which, ever since this period, has almost exclusively dominated the content and practice of philosophy in the English-speaking academies (while Bergson's name continues to evoke a titter which echoes all the way back to the halls of Cambridge). As Russell employs the consistency of the mathematical continuum as a means to disprove the existence of any substantial continuity or duration, returning to 'The Philosophy of Bergson' represents an ideal position from which to re-evaluate the logic of representation.

As early as *The Principles of Mathematics*, Russell condemned any appeals to the intuitive in the definition of continuity, declaring it a 'mass of unanalysed prejudice'. So when he encounters Bergson ten years later, announcing that the real is an indivisible continuum incommensurable with mathematical continuity, Russell not only declares the intuition of continuity an illusion, he goes as far as to say that 'throughout his account of duration, Bergson is unconsciously assuming the ordinary mathematical time; without this, his statements are unmeaning' (Russell 1912: 333). While 30 years later in his *History of Western Philosophy*, Russell announces that

> 'Continuity' had been, until [Cantor] defined it, a vague word, convenient for philosophers like Hegel, who wished to introduce metaphysical muddles into mathematics. Cantor gave a precise significance to the word, and showed that continuity, as he defined it, was the concept needed by mathematicians and physicists. By this means a great deal of mysticism, such as that of Bergson, was rendered antiquated. (Russell 1961: 783)

This stance is characteristic of twentieth-century Anglo-American thought, where through the advances of science, mathematics and logic, modernity made a break from philosophy 'muddled by experience'. Even today, it is generally accepted as given that, despite problems surrounding its definition, the real number continuum constitutes the foundation of time.

Russell's critique of Bergson focuses on two of the foundational problems of the analytic tradition: the definitions of number and continuity. In *Time and Free Will* Bergson had argued that number is inherently spatial and inapplicable to continuous phenomena and, through an interpretation of Zeno's paradoxes, that the mathematical conception of continuity is incommensurable with the duration of movement and change. Russell contends that in both cases Bergson's arguments merely present 'traditional errors' in number theory and mathematics to portray the limitations of the intellect, concluding that it is Bergson's intellect which is deficient, not the faculty itself. Through a paraphrase of Frege, Russell aims to show that number is not spatial but a purely logical entity, and through his own solution to the paradoxes of Zeno, derived from Cantor's set theory, he endeavours to invalidate Bergson's claim that continuity is irreducible to a discrete series.

Although Russell's critique of Bergson is, as Milec Capek puts it, unashamedly 'malicious' and presents a limited and distorted view of his work, it offers a means of examining the shortcomings of the analytical approach. Both Frege's logical foundation of number and

Cantor's conception of mathematical continuity have been shown to be less consistent than Russell believed them to be, verifying Bergson's more intuitive apprehensions. Most importantly, ensuing efforts to remedy Cantor's continuum hypothesis were not only shown to be fruitless, they unexpectedly revealed the existence of a common element to all computational, algorithmic or, in Bergson's terms, 'intellectual' procedures. Moreover, this definition of the intellect reveals that the algorithmic neither accounts for the whole of thought nor is it entirely commensurable with the continuity of process. Retrospectively, in attempting to make a comedy of Bergsonism, Russell not only produced a precise definition of the intellect but equally validated the limitations Bergson attributed to it.

The second chapter of *Time and Free Will* provides a description of number's origin in the synthetic unity of the intellect. Bergson's argument closely resembles the analysis of number in Aristotle's *Metaphysics* where, for example, number is said to be a potential quality of the numbered which is actualized in thought. The being of number, in this sense, in contrast to the Platonic conception of number as that which is logically prior to and distinct from the numbered, lies solely in consciousness and is, Aristotle writes, 'in itself not the substance of anything' (*Metaphysics*, p. 1088a). Departing from Aristotle, however, Bergson contends that in order to determine difference number relies on the properties of space. The unity of consciousness is the origin of the 'one', in the sense of a whole or a totality, but this unity is synthetic or presupposes a multiplicity: 'When we assert that number is a unit, we understand by this that we master the whole of it by a simple and indivisible intuition of the mind; this unity thus includes a multiplicity, since it is the unity of the whole' (Bergson 1919: 80). Not to be confused with the intuition defined in later works, this 'indivisible intuition' is the synthetic unity of the intellect itself. Using number as evidence, Bergson aims to show that the intellect is predicated on spatial distinction. As number further illustrates, the spatial nature of the intellect applies not only to the process of thought but also to the concepts it employs. In the case of number, Bergson points out that since individual differences are elided when numbering a set of elements, space becomes the means of separating the identical units as well as collecting them as a whole. Spatial distinction, in this respect, underlies the idea of a set and applies not only to the actual numbering of things but determines number in the abstract.

In 'The Philosophy of Bergson' Russell critiques the description of number outlined in *Time and Free Will*, drawing heavily on Frege's *Grundlagen der Arithmetik*, one of the foundational texts of the analytic tradition. In the *Grundlagen*, Frege set out to derive a definition of number from logic alone and exclude what he termed 'psychologism' from mathematics. This involved developing a definition of number through analysis alone without having recourse either to the Kantian idea of a synthetic a priori concept or to the things that numbers number. Frege achieved this by abstracting the idea of a number class from what specific numbers denote. He defined, for example, the number five as the class distinct from any collection of five things. The number 'five', in this case, is regarded as the class which all collections of five things partake, while the 'number' five is the 'class of all classes' of five things. Frege argued that number can never be given in itself because it is the purely logical object which allows us to think numbers in the first place. Hence he considered number in itself to be something devoid of spatial location: 'We can form no idea of number either as a self-subsistent object or as a property in an external thing, because number is in fact neither anything sensible nor a property of external things' (Frege 1950: 70). Frege argued that number is a purely logical property which can only be sensed in thought and is incapable of being an object of thought. It is this idea that number is a purely logical property, distinct from both perception and space that Russell inherits from Frege. From this perspective, Russell considers Bergson's contention that number is determined by and reflects the spatial nature of reflective consciousness to be patently naïve.

Bergson's account of number does suffer from some ambiguity, for example, the idea that synthetic unity and spatial distinction determine number is clouded somewhat by references to the necessity of picturing numbered things in order to discern number's spatial origins. However, these do not contradict the basic argument. We find in this instance, along with the birth of the analytic tradition, the emergence of the oppositional style of argument that accompanies it and which is still very much alive today. The problem with this approach is that it invariably assumes and constructs a unified image of the other which leaves no room for subtlety and elides points of possible agreement. This is clearly the case with Russell's critique, where, in typical style, he declares that Bergson 'does not know what number is, and has himself no clear idea of it' (Russell 1912: 328). He complains that Bergson has confused the distinction between the things numbered, numbers and number in general:

> Before we can be said to have any understanding of the number 12, we must know what different collections of twelve units have in common, and this is something which cannot be pictured because it is abstract. Bergson only succeeds in making his theory of number plausible by confusing a particular collection with the number of its terms, and this again with number in general. (Russell 1912: 329)

Russell insists that although we can picture numbers and, in some cases, we can picture what they number, we can under no circumstances picture *number* itself, since it is the logical property through which we understand 'numbers' in the first place. This, however, contradicts neither Bergson's essential claim that *numbering* is spatial nor the idea that number originates with the unity of reflective consciousness. In order to make his point Russell conducts a little creative misreading. Whereas Bergson considers number to originate with the unity of reflective consciousness, Russell interprets him as stating it is derived *from* actual objects given in space. This then becomes the basis for denouncing Bergson's argument that number is essentially spatial. Since Frege had shown number classes to precede actual numbers, number can never be given *in* space. Moreover, if number were derived from the numbering of actual things, Russell questions how he and Frege could have attained their ideas of number classes:

> The instance of number shows that, if Bergson were in the right, we could never have attained to the abstract ideas which are supposed to be thus impregnated with space; and conversely, the fact that we can understand abstract ideas (as opposed to particular things which exemplify them) seems sufficient to prove that he is

wrong in regarding the intellect as impregnated with space. (Russell 1912: 330)

In the end, Russell dismisses the idea that the intellect is fundamentally spatial on the grounds that the logic of classes is not derived from the numbering of actual things. However, rather than contradict the analysis of number in *Time and Free Will*, Russell in fact clarifies it. The distinction between things numbered and the set which corresponds to their number itself relies on spatial distinction. As Bergson points out:

It is not enough to say that number is a collection of units; we must add that these units are identical with one another, or at least that they are assumed to be identical when they are counted . . . Hence we may conclude that the idea of number implies the simple intuition of a multiplicity of parts and units, which are absolutely alike. (Bergson 1919: 76)

As each element in a class is considered identical there must be some means for their being differentiated. With a set of five things the set not only signifies the whole but the space between each element. The unity of the set derives from the synthetic unity of consciousness which cannot be pictured, for it is the frame which determines the set in the first place. With numbering, a common quality is attributed to the set which elides the singular differences of each element:

No doubt we can count the sheep in a flock and say that there are fifty, although they are all different from one another and are easily recognized by the shepherd: but the reason is that we agree in that case to neglect their individual differences and to take into account only what they have in common. (Bergson 1919: 76)

This common quality is the name and what set theory defined was simply the basis of denotation. The word 'sheep' signifies all sheep, irrespective of their singular differences. The name is determined by the synthetic unity of consciousness, where a quality is predicated to the abstract frame of perception, giving it the form of a class. The 'class of all classes' of five things, on the other hand, is the name of the number itself where the number defines its own class. In this respect, five is the quality predicated to all sets of five things, irrespective of their content.

Rather than showing the class of all classes to be logical and therefore not spatial, the fact that the name or the number appears to precede the naming and numbering of actual things reveals even abstraction to be purely spatial. The class of all classes is reflective consciousness in itself, and obviously cannot be made the object of reflection, because it is reflection. The class itself appears *sub specie aeternitatis* because it is nothing but the purely spatial frame of consciousness, revealing space and abstraction to be the same thing.

The origin of the class concept or the idea of a set in the unity of reflective consciousness was confirmed by Russell himself. Given the idea of a set is the unity of consciousness, any attempt to reduce number purely to a logic of classes will inevitably confront the problem of self-referentiality. In keeping with this, Russell found contradictions to arise with the idea of a 'set of all sets', producing as a result what has come to be known as 'Russell's paradox'. For example, he asked whether 'the set of all sets that are not members of themselves' is a member of itself or not? If it is, he discovered, then it isn't; if it isn't, then it is. This contradiction within the idea of a set meant that Frege's reduction of number solely to the analysis of classes was no longer consistent, leading Frege to abandon the project of the *Grundlagen* completely.

In response to the paradoxes he discovered within the set theoretical definition of number, Russell developed a theory of types which aimed to preclude such things as a set being a member of itself. But this meant, among other things, that the theory of types extended to infinity, a problem already foreseen in Plato's *Parmenides* with the paradox of the 'third man'. As Parmenides points out, 'if man is the form of men, then there must be a form for both man and men, and a form for the form for both man and men, and so on, *ad infinitum*'. The paradox of infinite regress simply results from the vain attempt to objectify the 'unity' which objectivity presupposes. As Kant argued, the synthetic will always haunt mathematics (Kant 1993: 37ff). As set theory has revealed, it will also plague any attempts to reduce the origin of language and meaning to analysis alone.

The spatial and therefore eternal nature of linguistic meaning, number and the class concept, expose both the Platonism inherent in number and language and the origin of Platonism in the structure of reflective consciousness. As Bergson writes, 'it may be said that, in a certain sense, we are all born Platonists' (Bergson 1983: 49). The unity of reflective consciousness, the abstract ego or whatever name one wishes to give to it, has and produces the sense of eternity. Consciousness, in this respect, is 'disembodied', arising at the expense of the duration of affective awareness and memory. It is no surprise that by supposedly excluding the 'psychological' from logic and mathematics, Russell and Frege were obliged to adopt a form of mathematical Platonism. Frege considered the sense of number to arise through a sort of anamnesis, where in order to conceive of numbers we must participate in a Platonic 'third realm'. Russell's entire analytical project is predicated on beliefs such as the logic of classes preceding the empirical understanding of actual numbers. What they both demonstrate is the common origin of mathematics, Platonism and theology. The class concept in general is purely 'spatial', in the sense that it exists outside of both time and matter, revealing mathematical Platonism to be indistinguishable from Judaeo-Christian theology – where the 'third realm' is the mathematician's heaven.

The view that logical and mathematical 'objects' have an independent existence remains a common assumption in the philosophy of mathematics. Roger Penrose, for example, continues to think in the tradition of Russell, insisting that mathematical objects are timeless:

There is something absolute and 'God-given' about mathematical truth. That is what mathematical Platonism is all about. Any particular formal system has a provisional and 'man-made' quality about it. Such systems indeed have very valuable roles to play in mathematical discussions, but they can supply only a partial (or approximate) guide to truth. Real mathematical truth goes beyond these man-made constructions. (Penrose 1988: 508)

What Platonism fails to see is that the 'logical' is, so to speak, the 'psyche'. Both space and abstraction share the same origin as the unity of reflective consciousness. Accordingly, mathematical ideas must be seen to be created as much as material form. On the other hand, eternity is part of the very nature of mathematics, since the abstract can be nothing but timeless. As Bergson points out, the class of nothing Frege discerns as the basis of number, is predicated on the negation of some thing. Exactly as Nietzsche described theology, mathematics is elevated to the transcendental, at the expense of life and thought. In the eyes of both theology and Platonism, this life is forever destined to be a poor copy of a model eternity. This, however, is precisely how Russell thought philosophy should be.

> A philosophical proposition must be such as can be neither proved nor disproved by empirical evidence. Too often we find in philosophical books arguments based upon the course of history, or the convolutions of the brain, or the eyes of shell-fish. Special and accidental facts of this kind are irrelevant to philosophy which must make only such assertions as would be equally true however the actual world were constituted. (Russell 1918: 107)

Ironically, Russell himself was to eventually abandon such Platonic ideals for philosophy. More insidious though is the current trend, exemplified by Penrose, in which the laws of physics are employed as a guide to the true workings of the mind. From this perspective, there is no aspect of thought that cannot be represented while chaos emerges as the motor of creativity; making the Mandelbrot set a work of art. With logic and science being so complex, challenges to such views are kept at bay by the fear of mathematics. On the other hand, fuelled by the fear that anything other than reason can only be disorder, there is a tendency within Anglo-American philosophy and science towards the dogmatic defence of 'truth'.

INFINITE AND INFINITIVE

Although Planck's constant suggests a limit to the divisibility of matter, the infinite divisibility of time and number renders any 'frame' to be arbitrary: units of time and measurement are, as Bergson writes, only ever 'provisionally final' (Bergson 1983: 154). Since any unit is arbitrary, there are no absolute boundaries distinguishing material modes in space or time. As the paradoxes of Zeno reveal, the infinite divisiblity of time, space and number also problematizes their continuity. Zeno demonstrated that since the flight of an arrow is infinitely divisible it never gets a chance to fly. Rather than proving movement illusory, the infinitesimal represents the idealism of the instant and the impossibility of fully actualizing pure perception. In the end, the paradox shows us that the point where the arrow is motionless is precisely the pure infinitive of duration itself.

Zeno's paradoxes also prove that mathematical time and the continuity of substantial duration within which the arrow of time is immanent are different in kind. The 'resolution' of Zeno's paradox with the continuity of movement is, therefore, a false problem. Throughout his oeuvre, Bergson employs the paradoxes of Zeno to demonstrate the intellect's inability to conceive of motion as other than a series of discrete states and the impossibility of representing the absolute duration or *mobility* of movement and change. In one sense, Bergson concurs with Zeno's contention that at each point on its trajectory, for example, an arrow must be at rest and that this inevitably leads to the conclusion that motion does not exist. In contrast to Zeno, however, Bergson holds that the paradoxes apply not to movement *per se* but solely to its representation: all that any of the paradoxes present us with is the representation of motion as a series of discrete states and the trajectory of each movement, but not movement in itself. The paradox arises from the assumption that movement and its trajectory are the same thing:

> It is to [the] confusion between motion and the space traversed that the paradoxes of the Eleatics are due; for the interval which separates two points is infinitely divisible, and if motion consisted of parts like those of the interval itself, the interval would never be crossed. (Bergson 1919: 112–13)

Zeno's paradox concerns not the 'flight' of the arrow, what Bergson terms absolute mobility, but its trajectory. It equally relates to the data by which we represent motion, revealing its incommensurability with the infinitive of movement to indicate a dimension of substantial duration beyond the limits of scientific representation.

The confusion between the continuity of movement and the space traversed has meant that ever since Zeno the problem of continuity has plagued Western philosophy. As a means of maintaining the actuality of movement and change, Aristotle proposed that the divisibility of space and time was potentially infinite. Although all this really meant was that the paradoxes were unsolvable, it worked as a bandaid until the arrival of the calculus. In this case, the infinite divisibility of numerical continuity problematized the idea of a continuous function, leaving mathematics without a solid foundation. Leibniz and Newton proposed limits to division in the form of the infinitesimal and the fluxion respectively, but these did little more than offer alternative names for the potentially infinite. In the nineteenth century, however, Cantor produced a definition of the mathematical continuum employing arithmetic alone, which demonstrated the actuality, rather than potentiality, of the mathematical continuum.

Cantor's definition of the mathematical continuum is derived from an arithmetic of sets. He first defined continuity as a 'set of points' and then developed a method for determining the numerical 'size' of the continuum without recourse to counting. Rather than having to count sets independently, Cantor showed that one need only map one set onto the other: in the sense that by pairing them off, a set of cups can be shown to be the same size as a set of saucers. He argued that there is no reason why this one-to-one correspondence cannot be extended to *infinite* sets, such as the 'set of natural numbers'. Using this method, Cantor discovered that although the even or odd numbers appeared intuitively smaller than the natural numbers, when put in one-to-one correspondence they were equivalent in size.

The next step was to establish the size of the continuum which, as the set of real numbers or 'points on a line', would be the same as the set of all possible subsets of the natural numbers. Since the set of all the subsets belonging to a set, or the *power set*, has a greater cardinal size than the set itself, the aim was to show that the real number continuum was larger than the set of natural numbers. He proposed that if the set of real numbers is *not* larger than the set of natural numbers, or if the set of real numbers is *countable*, then the real numbers can be put in one-to-one correspondence with the set of natural numbers. Cantor then showed this to be false by constructing a means of producing a real number that could *not* be paired off with the natural or counting numbers, revealing in the process the set of all subsets of the natural numbers to be the cardinal 'size' of the continuum.

Due to continuity being the infinite *succession* of real numbers, the *cardinal* magnitude of the continuum needs to be ordered. What is now known as the 'continuum hypothesis' asks if the arbitrary set of real numbers can be defined as an ordered series. The question itself is derived from Cantor's construction of what he termed 'transfinite ordinals' (Cantor 1899). In this case, Cantor extended the idea of an ordinal series, generated from the successive addition of units in a particular order, into the infinite by assigning a number which signified the order of any unlimited series, and then generating an ordinal sequence of 'transfinite' ordinal numbers. The solution to the question, Is the set of all sets of natural numbers equal to the sequence of sequences of natural numbers? then becomes the continuum itself.

Cantor's definition of mathematical continuity had a major impact on Russell, determining both the content and direction of his thought almost from the beginning. Although Cantor himself had some reservations concerning the consistency of his analysis and its direct application to reality, Russell took little haste in declaring it a complete success. For instance, with characteristic confidence he announces in *The Principles of Mathematics*:

> The chief reason for the elaborate and paradoxical theories of space and time and their continuity, which have been constructed by philosophers, has been the supposed contradictions in a continuum composed of elements . . . Cantor's continuum is free from contradictions. (Russell 1964: 347)

Accepting that continuity could be defined as a discrete series solely through logical analysis, without appealing to either the empirical or intuitive for validation, Russell believed Cantor had established not only an ontological basis to science but the scientific status of philosophy. Following from his belief that number as an abstract class logically precedes the actual numbering of things, Russell concluded from Cantor's definition of the continuum as the class of real numbers that the mathematical continuum must be prior to our 'intuitions' of spatial, material and temporal continuity. Although Cantor's definition of the mathematical continuum proved to be less consistent than Russell's tenacity, that continuity and, as a consequence, time is a discrete series, remains a virtually unchallenged assumption in contemporary science and philosophy. Alongside this is the almost universal presumption that any appeals to an intuitive temporality are simply veiled forms of mysticism.

With the aid of Cantor's definition of continuity Russell proposed a 'solution' to the paradoxes of Zeno which has since become standard. His first step was to replace the idea of an 'intuitive' whole, corresponding to a period of motion, with the concept of an 'intensional' whole which signifies the class of real numbers. From Russell's perspective, the problem with Zeno's approach is that it presupposes the enumeration of steps or divisions and, as a consequence, an entity which is necessarily finite. An intensional whole, on the other hand, is determined by the class which defines it, meaning that infinite collections can be established without the need to enumerate all finite members (Russell 1964: 349–50). Once this is done, the flight of the arrow, for example, can be defined as a mathematical series by giving the target the value of the limit of an *actually infinite* series of positions. So if the arrow traverses a distance from zero to one mile, 'one mile' represents the limit of the journey, the limit itself being the equivalent of the infinite expression of the mathematical series of distances it traverses. Since this set can be defined 'intensionally', the actual enumeration of the infinite series need not be carried out, as the limit defines the infinite series as a class.

Since Bergson had employed Zeno's paradoxes as a means of demonstrating the disjunction between continuity and representation, in 'The Philosophy of Bergson' Russell considers his resolution of the paradoxes reason enough to reject entirely Bergson's account of the continuity of duration. He further rejects Bergson's claim that change occurs within the infinitive of its unfolding, arguing that the paradoxes reveal there is no continuous state of change while his own solution to them proves that change is a continuous series of states. In all, Russell's critique aims to reject entirely any idea of continuity which would conflict either with the image of matter presupposed by science or with scientific concepts, such as the calculus. In this respect, Russell's point of view is very much in keeping with the contemporary episteme where the assumption that science and the scientific method gives us an unmediated perception of the real continues to reign. Accordingly, any attempts to characterize scientific thought or define its limits and limitations are met with charges of irrationalism.

Rather than contradict Bergson's critique of the mathematical representation of continuity, Russell simply takes it to its infinite extreme. By defining continuity as the set of real numbers, movement is reduced solely to the trajectory of the object and time is rendered indistinguishable from the space traversed. Although the real number continuum is presupposed by measurement in general, as well as any continuous mathematical function, it is predicated on the absolute idealism of the instant. The instant, however necessary it may be to scientific representation and analysis, has never been, and never will be, given to experience or established anywhere outside of thought. No matter how accurate a measuring device or atomic clock may be, the instant remains an impossible limit. The real number continuum represents the absolute limit and ground of representation. On the other hand, the instant conditions scientific thought and representation in its entirety, introducing a Platonism into science which is, as Bergson writes, 'immanent to the method' (Bergson 1983: 345).

NUMBER AND MULTIPLICITY

The synthetic unity which makes the apprehension of the field of perception a given whole is the same as that which enables equally infinite objects, such as the natural or real numbers, to be conceived as a totality. Since the whole can only be given in thought and, as Kant made clear, cannot be made an object of thought, any objective totality will always be an element of a greater whole and for this reason can never be said to be complete. This is equally the case when determining the continuum: as soon as it is defined objectively as the set of all sets of natural numbers, for example, it becomes part of an even greater set. In a figurative sense the infinite series of infinities that arises from Cantor's set theory leads asymptotically to the union of subject and object, or immanence.

Not surprisingly, soon after its inception Cantor's continuum was unsettled by a number of self-referential paradoxes. However, it is not often advertised that Cantor not only encountered problems in the definition of the continuum prior to Russell's discovery of the paradox of the 'set of all sets' but proposed solutions. This might have something to do with Cantor being something of a devout Spinozist. He believed, for one, that his definition of the continuum described extension as an actually infinite *Transfinitum* which he then equated with Spinoza's *natura naturata* (Dauben 1979: 145). That is, he considered the modes of extension or products of nature to be 'actually infinite'. In Spinozism *natura naturata* must be considered an *actual infinity* in order to maintain its distinction from *natura naturans* or nature as an indivisible continuum.

As the example of the calculus suggests, that the real number continuum is an actual rather than a potential infinity is presupposed in order for calculation to work. Although infinite division renders any scientific unit arbitrary, determining a unit equally assumes that there is a limit to division:

> . . . the intellect represents *becoming* as a series of *states*, each of which is homogenous with itself and consequently does not change. Is our attention called to the internal change of one of these states? At once we decompose it into another series of states which, reunited, will be supposed to make up this internal modification. Each of these new states must be invariable, or else their internal change, if we are forced to notice it, must be resolved again into a fresh series of invariable states, and so on to infinity. Here again, thinking consists in reconstituting, and, naturally, it is with *given* elements, and consequently with *stable* elements, that we reconstitute. (Bergson 1983: 163)

The continuity that eludes representation in the end undoes any idea of a whole or totality. All totalities and 'closed sets' are open to the continuity through which they evolve. Accordingly, atomism does not go as far as the intellect would have it. 'Pure perception' is assumed in the determination of objective data and in the frame through which discrete images are isolated as units, but the continuity of duration renders all units provisional, 'partial expressions' of a whole which changes. From Bergson's perspective, it is duration which 'hinders everything from being given all at once', implying that *natura naturata* itself can no longer be considered a consistent totality (Bergson 1992: 93). This leads to the declaration, in *Creative Evolution*, that 'the real whole might well be, we conceive, an indivisible continuity' (Bergson 1983: 31).

In the first of the *Cinema* books, Giles Deleuze articulates the implications of bringing duration into the concept of the set. His reading of Bergson describes perfectly the fact that the impossibility of determining either a set of all sets or a highest ordinal implicates the whole within every set. The paradox of the set of all sets introduces an inconsistency into all 'sets' from the one to the highest cardinal. As Deleuze writes:

We know the insoluble contradictions we fall into when we treat the set of all sets as a whole. It is not because the notion of the whole is devoid of sense; but it is not a set and it does not have parts. It is rather that which prevents each set, however big it is, from closing in on itself, and that which forces it to extend itself into a larger set. The whole is therefore like a thread which traverses sets and gives each one the possibility, which is necessarily realized, of communicating with another, to infinity. (Deleuze 1986: 16–17)

As Deleuze alludes, Bergson's fundamental critique of the intellect is that it can only deal with partial entities or with 'closed' systems. Although Cantor's set theory was received as bringing consistency into mathematics, it has only served to direct the arrow back at itself, ultimately vindicating Bergson's critique of Zeno and the intellect.

In the analysis of number in *Time and Free Will*, Bergson reveals infinite division to be at the foundation of number itself, for it can be regarded either as an indivisible unity or as a multiplicity of divisions. 'One', for example, can be regarded as a whole or as an infinite sum of fractions. For this reason, the synthetic unity of the one *presupposes* a pre-existing multiplicity. In this regard, Bergson writes, the 'actual and not merely virtual perception of subdivisions in what is undivided is just what we call objectivity' (Bergson 1919: 84). In objectivity the numbered appears as a 'plurality', and each element of a plurality is itself infinitely divisible. At its limit, number presupposes an actual infinity of divisions. As Deleuze writes in *Bergsonism*: 'the objective *is that which has no virtuality*' (Deleuze 1991: 41). The numerical 'potential' of number is always *actual* to it. In this sense, the infinite divisibility of the numbered is the objective correlate of number.

Further to this, Bergson considers the isolation of a 'set' or a 'totality' to be always an abstraction from a larger 'whole'. Even the concept of matter as a totality is predicated on the idea of a 'frame' within which that whole is conceived. For this reason, matter must be regarded as 'actually infinite' not only in order to avoid false problems but also for the term 'matter' to have any significance. Although this actual infinity is a 'fiction', the presupposition that all is given, Bergson writes, is 'immanent to the method' of analysis (Bergson 1983: 345). In the sense that the real number continuum is a basic assumption in the use of the calculus, we must assume that there is a limit to division when we analyse objective processes.

The simplest example of this is the synthetic unity of reflective consciousness which cannot itself be made an object of reflective consciousness because it is the foundation of objectivity itself. Even though the real, as Bergson puts it, tends towards a discrete multiplicity of modes, the representation of any set of modes not only abstracts it from the indivisible continuity of process, it inevitably presents it as a multiple of the one. For this reason set theory is probably the clearest manifestation of the structure of reflective consciousness. The fact that the natural numbers can be referred to as a set simply demonstrates that the synthetic unity of reflective consciousness determines 'extensive' as well as 'intensive' apprehension. All that a concept such as the 'set of all natural numbers' signifies is that the idea of totality has no limit.

Prior to the difficulties that Russell discerned with the 'set of all sets', Cantor had intuited problems with his own definition of the continuum. However, he did not consider inconsistency as signalling a deficiency of logic, but where thought and substance part ways. In response to the limitations of set theory, Cantor proposed two distinct conceptions of multiplicity:

> If we start from the notion of a definite multiplicity [Vielheit] (a system, a totality) of things, it is necessary, as I discovered, to distinguish two kinds of multiplicities (by this I always mean *definite* multiplicities).
>
> For a multiplicity can be such that the assumption that *all* of its elements 'are together' leads to a contradiction, so that it is impossible to conceive of the multiplicity as a unity, as 'one finished thing'. Such multiplicities I call *absolutely infinite* or *inconsistent multiplicities*. (Cantor 1899: 114)

It is interesting to note that ten years prior to this, in the text that Russell condemned for its shoddy mathematics, Bergson had not only intuited the incommensurability between mathematical continuity and duration but had also argued for the recognition of the existence of two distinct multiplicities. In contrast to the closed sets that compose matter, Bergson proposes that duration is a *qualitative* multiplicity:

> In short, we must admit two kinds of multiplicity, two possible senses of the word 'distinguish', two conceptions, the qualitative and the other quantitative, of the difference between *same* and *other*. Sometimes this multiplicity, this distinctness, this heterogeneity contains number only potentially, as Aristotle would have said. Consciousness, then, makes a qualitative discrimination without any further thought of counting the qualities or even of distinguishing them as *several*. (Bergson 1919: 121)

Duration as a qualitative multiplicity is expressed through the apprehension and expression of affective difference. Affectivity's multiple nature gives a sense of difference which is neither spatial nor temporal but wholly substantial: it is expressed through a multiplicity which must be said to interpenetrate and whose only unity, as Deleuze points out, is its multiplicity (Deleuze 1991: 85). The unfolding of affective difference takes place solely within the absolute infinitive of its pure duration. In this sense, it is only through affectivity that the production of difference can be apprehended.

Moreover, with set theory and the distinction between quantitative and qualitative multiplicities, the ontological ground of Bergson's distinction between the objects of science and metaphysics can be discerned. As Bergson writes in *The Creative Mind*: 'Thus we have on the one hand science and mechanical art, which have to do with pure intellect; on the other hand, metaphysics, which calls upon intuition' (Bergson 1992: 79). Metaphysics begins, Bergson argues, at the limits of science. From Newtonian dynamics to fractal geometry and chaos theory, matter is regarded as atomistic and change is conceived outside the subject. Although quantum mechanics, for example, suggests an indivisible continuity coexists the atomistic model, the wave-function serves merely to bring 'unpredictability' into the 'discrete' realm of atomic positions. It is the external subject who renders continuity radically ulterior and all attempts to bring time into science, from Einstein to Prigogine, manage only to edge closer to the infinitive of experience. The metaphysics of time and change must begin from experience in order to determine that which can only be experienced. It is only within time that the duration of thought itself can be apprehended as well as expressed.

THE MECHANICS OF THOUGHT

The infinitive can be seen to appear not only at the limits of the mathematical conception of the continuum but also within the limits of logic and the logical definition of the thought process that emerged from Cantor's work. After problems arose in what David Hilbert termed 'Cantor's Paradise', one of the primary goals of what became known as formalist mathematics was the axiomatization of the set theoretical definition of the continuum. Russell and Whitehead's mammoth *Principia Mathematica* is one example of an attempt to get the logic straight and reduce mathematics to a fundamental collection of axioms. However, soon after the formalist programme began, Kurt Gödel came up with his 'incompleteness theorems'. Gödel comprehensively demonstrated that there were apparently 'true' statements in any formal system, such as set theory, which could not be proven so from within the system itself. Hilbert and Russell's plan to ground Cantorian set theory in formal logic was proven to be interminably incomplete. Gödel produced his demonstration by manipulating Cantor's diagonal method, which demonstrated the existence of a real number not containable in the set of natural numbers, to show that in order to prove the consistency of one axiom another would need to be added, and so on. Platonism once again stumbled on the third-man argument; in order to prove an axiom another would have to be produced but the same 'incompleteness' would remain, requiring another axiom, and so on, *ad infinitum*. Gödel in the end declared that neither the synthetic nor the intuitive could be banished from either mathematics or logic, ratifying Bergson's claim that the limitations of intellectual processes are 'immanent to the method' of the intellect itself, and are incapable of being objectified.

Another problem that Hilbert raised was what is known as the *Entscheidungsproblem*. This enquired as to whether or not there existed a mechanical process applicable to any mathematical statement that could answer if that statement were provable or not. The problem came down to asking if there was a definite method for solving mathematical problems (Hodges 1988: 4). If the answer was affirmative then a general algorithm for answering all mathematical problems could be said to exist, but if it could be proven that some problem had no algorithmic solution, then the *Entscheidungsproblem* would itself be unsolvable. In a paper entitled, 'On Computable Numbers, with an Application to the *Entscheidungsproblem*', Alan Turing approached this question by first defining in a precise sense the intuitive ideas of algorithmic or mechanical processes. He began by considering the calculation of computable real numbers: those numbers whose infinite decimal expansion is calculable by finite means (Turing 1936: 116). Turing reduced the process by which the abstract subject computed the problem to an unlimited pad or 'tape' upon which the calculation proceeded, a finite number of symbols, a set of instructions and a discrete series of computational steps. He was then able to show that whatever a human could compute could be carried out by a 'machine' configured in the same manner. The class of computable numbers is then shown to be 'denumerable' in the Cantorian sense, that is, equivalent to the class of natural numbers. Turing then applied Cantor's diagonal method to demonstrate the existence of real numbers which cannot be computed by any machine, that is, which are 'uncomputable'.

Turing produced conclusive evidence that Hilbert's problem was false, in as much as there was no general algorithm for proving mathematical problems. But in the process he produced what is now the founding document of discussions about 'Artificial Intelligence'. His argument extended to the conclusion that 'it is possible to invent a single machine which can be used to compute any computable sequence' (Turing 1936: 127). From one point of view, Turing argued that any mechanical process could be coded by a 'Turing Machine'. From another, his findings suggested that all intellectual processes are inherently algorithmic or mechanistic. In both cases 'mechanical process' is defined simply in terms of the iteration of discrete states. The resulting conception of 'mechanical intelligence' is practically isomorphic to Bergson's description of the intellect as a mechanism in *Creative Evolution*. Bergson's 'pure intellect' is the *abstract* process of computation which represents processes as discrete series of given elements or symbols. Accordingly, the 'Turing Machine' can be regarded as the precise definition of Bergson's 'pure intellect' as a faculty. Further to this, in the same year that Turing published 'On Computable Numbers' papers were published by Gödel, Alonzo Church, Stephen Kleene and Emil Post, which all offered independent demonstrations of the existence of an abstract 'algorithmic process'. However, not one of these examples is considered as 'proof'. As Turing himself notes:

> The expression 'there is a general process for determining . . .' has been used throughout this section as equivalent to 'there is a machine which will determine . . .' This usage can be justified if and only if we can justify our definition of 'computable' . . . All arguments which can be given are bound to be, fundamentally, appeals to intuition, and for this reason rather unsatisfactory mathematically. (Turing 1936: 134–5)

Accordingly, terms such as 'effectively computable', 'recursive function' or 'Turing Machine computable' must be regarded more as intuitive hypotheses than formal definitions, as in line with Gödel's findings, computation cannot be defined in itself. However, the independent and simultaneous expression of equivalent processes through different formal means is generally regarded as evidence that these hypotheses are correct. The various results can be collectively regarded, in Spinozist terms, as the expression of a 'common notion' of an 'immanent' idea. We literally cannot define the ground of the intellect in intellectual terms, which is why Bergson identifies all 'purely intellectual' processes as expressive of a general 'tendency' of thought immanent to the formal products of the intellect:

> All the operations of our intellect tend to geometry, as to the goal where they find their perfect fulfillment. But, as geometry is necessarily prior to them (since these operations have not as their end to construct space and cannot do otherwise than take it as given), it is evident that it is a latent geometry, immanent in our idea of space, which is the mainspring of our intellect and the cause of its working. (Bergson 1983: 210–11)

Bergson is careful to distinguish this 'latent geometry' from the Kantian intuitions; geometry is employed here simply as a trope for the identity principle which is at the basis of mechanical repetition. Again, it is this relation which underlies both the intellect as a mechanism of thought and its abstract and formal products. The fundamental characteristics of the Bergsonian intellect are, first, its reliance on the abstraction of discrete states from continuous processes and, second, the contraction of a continuous relation throughout the discrete series. For this reason, Bergson argues that intellectual, and by extension mechanical, processes are inherently deterministic. In a paper entitled 'Computing Machinery and Intelligence' Turing defines 'intelligence' in precisely these terms:

> . . . digital computers . . . may be classified among the 'discrete state machines'. These are the machines which move by sudden jumps or clicks from one quite different state to another. These sudden states are sufficiently different for the possibility of confusion between them to be ignored. *Strictly speaking there are no such machines. Everything really moves continuously.* But there are many kinds of machines which can profitably be thought of as being discrete state machines . . . It will seem that given the initial state of the machine and the input signals it is always possible to predict

all future states. This is reminiscent of Laplace's view that from the complete state of the universe at one moment in time, as described by the positions and velocities of all particles, it should be possible to predict all future states. The prediction which we are considering is, however, rather nearer to practicability than that considered by Laplace. The system of the 'universe as a whole' is such that quite small errors in the initial conditions can have an overwhelming effect at a later time. The displacement of a single electron by a billionth of a centimetre at one moment might make the difference between a man being killed by an avalanche a year later, or escaping. *It is an essential property of the mechanical systems which we have called 'discrete state machines' that this phenomenon does not occur.* Even when we consider the actual physical machines instead of the idealised machines, reasonable accurate knowledge of the state at one moment yields reasonable accurate knowledge any number of steps later. (Turing 1950: 11–12, my emphasis)

Although with the advent of high-speed computation 'discrete state machines' have proved capable of modelling the butterfly effect, this does not alter the fact that computer programs remain, as Georg Kampis describes it, 'complexity-preserving'. More importantly, in the above Turing clearly recognizes the disjunction between the continuity of both thought and dynamical processes and the intellect as a 'discrete-state mechanism'. As with Bergson's conception of the intellect as a mechanism, the definition of 'machine intelligence' is predicated on the *negation* of continuity and the *abstraction* of a symbolically defined system from the 'universe as a whole'. As Bergson writes in *Creative Evolution*:

The mechanistic explanations . . . hold good for the systems that our thought artificially detaches from the whole. But of the whole itself and of the systems which, within this whole, seem to take after it, we cannot admit *a priori* that they are mechanically explicable, for then time would be useless, and even unreal. The essence of mechanical explanation, in fact, is to regard the future and the past as calculable functions of the present, and thus to claim that *all is given*. (Bergson 1983: 37)

As Turing points out, the combined effects of negation and abstraction remove uncertainty from the continuity of process. Bergson equally considers the Laplacian ideal of infinite information to be 'immanent to the method' of the intellect as a mechanism of thought. Since the determination of a 'discrete state' is predicated on process being 'stopped for an instant', that which eludes the grasp of the intellect as a mechanism, and the mechanistic models of processes, is the duration of process itself. Mechanism is the limit of the intellect's involvement with process, meaning that we can only objectively conceive and logically or mathematically deduce from what has gone before what might happen again. In keeping with this, Bergson argues that 'matter' as an 'aggregate of images' is derived from 'the suppression of all efficient duration, the likening of the universe to a thing *given*, which a superhuman intelligence would embrace at once in a moment or eternity' (Bergson 1983: 346). This 'superhuman' perspective is that given with objectivity and is embodied in the 'mechanical' subject who performs mathematical equations or who simply 'computes'. As Brian Rotman has argued, this 'superhuman' perspective is the disembodied 'ghost' in Turing's machine (Rotman 1993).

The proximity of the Turing Machine to the pure intellect is an affirmation of Bergson's *positive* categorization of the intellect as a 'faculty'. The discovery of a general form of intellectual thought only vindicates Bergson's fundamental claim that 'The intellect is not made to think *evolution*, in the proper sense of the word – that is to say, the continuity of a change that is pure mobility' (Bergson 1983: 163). As with Turing, Bergson contends that if we are to conceive the world as 'given', or think of movement objectively as a series of discrete states, then the continuity of thought and process is elided. However, Bergson argues that the 'indeterminacy' which undermines mechanism is simply a trope for that which the intellect *cannot think*. 'Indeterminacy' and 'disorder' are terms which include the determinate and order and merely indicate that which lies beyond the frame of the intellect (Bergson 1983: 222). Alternatively, in order to apprehend the duration of change or 'evolution' we must bring continuity into what is considered to be the process of thought.

THE LOGIC OF THINKING

While we tend to make a number of discrete acts and decisions, the vast majority of our actions, thoughts and encounters take place within the undivided continuity of our unreflective consciousness. It is within the duration of our affective consciousness that we act in response to desires and external influences, and it is also with this continuity that we apprehend and produce the qualitative or aesthetic differences that colour our being in the world. Although arising from a material 'cause', for instance, and 'mechanically' perceived by the senses, nerves and brain, 'tastes' cannot be entirely reduced to the chemical composition of the foods we eat. Similarly, when listening to music, the discrete notes alone do not make up the melody. Music is apprehended continuously, and the melody transforms as proceeding notes are enfolded into one another in what is received as a continuous *affective* modulation. The same continuity can be said of the processes of writing, painting, cooking, social interaction and, possibly, change itself.

As Bergson has pointed out, the immediacy of our affective duration is not simply an illusion but is in fact the direct expression of the continuity of thought. It is through an affective sensibility that music, literature and art are both communicated and created. While music can certainly be represented through notation, the score obviously does not represent the music, which can only be apprehended. Deriving from more than simply the material, aesthetic differences emerge from the continuous or living movement of cultural and collective sensibility.

From this perspective, the material, ideally actualized body parallels but is qualitatively distinct from the enduring mind. Thought and extension are, as Spinoza points out, distinct attributes of the same substance. Material bodies, forms, and the mathematical order that governs them certainly exist. However, there is more to life than simply form and order. As the case of art reveals, that which cannot be reduced to a sum of parts is composition. It is through the nature or logic of the process of composition that forms not only come into being but also interrelate. And it is here, not the nature of the pure and untouched, but the *naturing nature* of process that we can find the logic of continuity.

As Spinoza points out, the fact that existence is continuous means that causality must be immanent to the life or duration of substance. From this perspective, rather than that of the prime mover, God is the process of change itself. Spinoza, however, failed to see that substance is not determined but *determining*, that is, the movement and production of differences is a part of substance. In Spinoza's terminology, we now find that actual nature, or the movement of actuality is incommensurate with the 'nature' of substance or *natura naturans*. In order to transcend this disjunction we do not need to abandon science but shift the foundation of all practices from physics to metaphysics. As a consequence, the fundamental political task today is ontological. To complete it, philosophy must situate itself at the limit of scientific thought and distinguish the logic of actuality from the productive logic or nature of continuity.

Rather than presenting any 'given' form, nature represents the 'logic' of change and the production of differences. As Zeno's paradoxes suggest, and the Turing Machine also reveals, our representation of both change and thought differs in kind from the continuity in which change takes place. As Turing and others have argued, even mathematical reasoning requires a form of intuition in order to create new ideas. Creation, however, goes well beyond the mathematical and, while incapable of being apprehended objectively, remains ongoing in life as well as art. By apprehending the continuity of thought itself, it is possible to intuit the basis to an essentially 'productive' logic.

Ironically, Bergson's analysis of language and representation, and the manner in which it conditions what he termed the 'intellect', were furthered and ultimately confirmed by the findings and eventual failure of the Analytical project. The work of Gödel, Turing and Post, for instance, gives body to Bergson's account of the reflective thought process and an outline as to where intuition is fundamental to thought.

Bergson considers intuition to be at the origin of all 'intellectual' ideas. He finds the calculus, for example, to be derived from a fundamental intuition of the continuity of transformation. Although the intuition of the duration of change subsists in ideas such as Newton's 'fluxions', Bergson considers the intuitive element to have been lost when the calculus became reduced to the manipulation of 'symbols' (Bergson 1992: 33). This idea of an intuitive basis to mathematical thought is supported by Turing. In a paper based on his doctoral thesis, titled 'Systems of Logic Based on Ordinals', Turing argues that in 'post-Gödel' times it is impossible to find 'a formal logic which wholly eliminates the necessity of using intuition', adding that

> Mathematical reasoning may be regarded rather schematically as the exercise of two faculties, which we may call *intuition* and *ingenuity*. The activity of the intuition consists in making spontaneous judgements which are not the result of conscious trains of reasoning. (Turing 1965: 210)

Turing's idea of an originary intuition incommensurate with its symbolic representation receives further attention in the history of logic and machinic intelligence through the work of Emil Post. It is now accepted that Post anticipated the findings of Gödel and Turing by at least a decade (Davis (ed.), 1965: 338). Not only did he produce incompleteness and undecidability results comparable to Gödel's, he formulated a conception of 'finite combinatory processes' equivalent to Turing's 'computable numbers' which, most importantly, was expressed from the point of view of a 'worker' carrying out the computation. What is different about Post's work, however, and that which probably contributed to much of it being rejected for publication in his lifetime, is his conclusion that '*mathematical thinking is, and must remain, essentially creative*' (Post 1944: 316). Most of his analysis involved demonstrating that the *Principia Mathematica* was first a consistent deductive system and then, by application of the diagonal process, that it was by nature incomplete. He then showed that for any deductive system it was possible to produce another that was stronger, containing the former but producing more consistent statements (Post 1965: 416–17). Post regarded the 'creative' process of thought to be that which inheres in logical incompleteness and undecidability. Surprisingly, for a paper in logic, Post declares that his conclusion is more 'in line with Bergson's "Creative Evolution"' than Russell's *Principia* (Post 1965: 417).

As an appendix to the above paper, Post includes extracts from his notebooks and diary, giving a rough, intuitive account of the 'creative process'. In contradistinction to Turing's computer, which in being able to calculate infinite series has only a 'logical' existence, Post situates his worker in time. He argues that the process of computation is mostly unconscious, taking place in what he terms a 'psychic ether' which he compares to Bergson's 'theory of memory' (Post 1965: 432). From here, he argues that finite combinatory processes manipulate the spatialized symbolization of this unconscious creative process. It is the fact that creative thought is *continuous* which leads to a disjunction between mathematical processes and mathematical objects. Post then describes the movement between the continuity of process and discrete computation in explicitly Bergsonian terms; listing the stages in which ideas emerge as follows:

(a) Activity in time which is creative. This is the source of the process.
(b) By reflection this activity itself is frozen into spatial properties.
(c) The spatial relations are symbolized by spatial symbols.
(d) These symbols have no further symbolizable properties internally as it were and so end the descent. (This is essentially Bergsonian). (Post 1965: 420–21)

From Post's perspective, the 'computer' does not only perform algorithmic tasks, as in the case of the Turing Machine, it produces or 'creates' algorithms. As with both Turing and Bergson, who claim that 'everything really moves continuously', Post argues that the thought process is *continuous*. However, it is the continuity of thought which is lost in reflection, since the 'intellect' transforms temporal continuity into a series of 'spatial properties'. As with Brouwer's 'intuitionism', Post points out that it is the intuition of temporal order which has been neglected in symbolic logic and which gives rise to fallacies such as the greatest ordinal or the set of all sets. 'Incompleteness' and 'undecidability' are, for Post, expressions of the creativity or openness of mathematics and logic, which by nature elude reduction to axiomatization for they subsist in the duration of thought.

In a broad sense, although a finite combinatory process, or Turing Machine, can express a problem simply as the iteration of concrete operations irrespective of time or speed, the origin of each distinct 'machine' or algorithm originates in the intuition of a sense of temporal unfolding. It could be said that although the 'creative' in mathematics is literally the construction of algorithms, the creative 'process' is not itself algorithmic. Epistemologically, it is the subsistence of the intuitive ordering in time that cannot be completely formalized and which guarantees that formalization can never be completed. Post's account of this sense of a purely ordinal progression which precedes and is irreducible to its representation as a discrete series derives from Bergson's *Time and Free Will*. Here Bergson compares the qualitative ordering of time to musical variation, where differences blend into one another and the whole continuously transforms with each variation. As an example of this, he describes the subconscious cognition of the strokes of a clock where on the fourth stroke we become aware of the 'time'. Bergson then compares the relation of this subconscious perception to its apprehension in reflection:

> If, then, I question myself carefully on what has just taken place, I perceive that the first four sounds had struck my ear and even affected my consciousness, but that the sensations produced by each one of them, instead of being set side by side, had melted into one another in such a way as to give the whole a peculiar quality, to make a kind of musical phrase out of it. (Bergson 1919: 127)

The 'fourth' chime is apprehended as a qualitatively singular 'note', in this sense, not because of its difference from the previous sounds but from being enfolded within those that succeed. It is this purely qualitative and continuous sense of succession which expresses the immediate ground of our sense of duration, and it is that which allows us to differentiate 'times'. Moreover, this qualitative sense is irreducible to the simple numerical series given in reflection, as the fourth note, for example, expresses a singular intensity bound up in the duration in which it occurs.

In an essay entitled 'Intellectual Effort', Bergson outlines a model of the creative process of thought. Concerning the feeling we have of 'intellectual effort', he asks 'does not the consciousness of a certain . . . *movement of ideas* count for something?' (Bergson 1920: 186–7). He suggests that rather than bring to consciousness a given idea or static concept which is unchanged in expression, in the movement of thought a 'dynamic schema' or 'directive idea' is actualized which changes with and is implicated in each of its elements. Although this virtual 'schema' is given prior to its expression in the form of an 'image', it does not have a definite extension or direction. Image, in this case, can be said of any 'actual' element, a word in language, image in cinema, tone in music, ingredient in cuisine. In the first instance, the schema corresponds to an *expectation* of images' (Bergson 1920: 227). The initial sense of the idea is given in an intellectual tone, an affective disposition or feeling, and is the counterpart of what Bergson terms, in 'An Introduction to Metaphysics', the 'fluid concepts' inherent in intuition (Bergson 1992: 168). Since the initial idea or schema is transformed in the process of composition, for the images which are actualized modify the idea as it is expressed, the relations between images constitute the 'unforeseen' in composition (Bergson 1920: 213). Although the idea precedes its actualization, we have no idea what form it will take. The schema, in this sense, is virtual rather than 'possible', for its actualization is contingent on the elements through which it is expressed. It is only after it is actualized that the idea appears to precede its expression.

Intellectual 'effort' results from the resistance encountered from given modes of thought. This is due to the intellect being structured and limited by determinate concepts, the later forming the basis of habit and pragmatism. As the intellect, however, is the domain of language or signs in general, only it can provide the elements which will give form to the movement of thought. In line with this, Bergson describes the process of actualization as 'something intermediate . . . between the efficient cause and the final cause' (Bergson 1920: 230). The process of actualization is 'formative' rather than formal: while the 'schemata' condition the expression of thought, the relations between the elements through which it is expressed remain indeterminate. Moreover, the relation between actual and virtual is neither dialectical nor recursive: indetermination is implicated within the process of actualization and cannot be considered in isolation from the idea which expresses it. Accordingly, the transformation of thought can be conceived neither as a progression nor as a series of radical breaks. Bergson considers the evolution of thought to follow a 'succession without mutual externality' (Bergson 1919: 108). That conscious states are continuous and 'mutually interpenetrating' means that there can be no difference between before and after in which to conceive of a 'progression'. In other words, we cannot say where one thought ends and another begins.

Bergson equally considers the virtual and actual, the dynamic schema and its materialization, to 'differ in kind'. The formative idea is not only irreducible to the material form in which it is expressed, it can be manifest in a potential multiplicity of modes. While thought is generally expressed in 'pre-exisiting elements', the subject, as Bergson points out:

> . . . can almost arbitrarily choose the first elements of the group provided that the others are complementary to them; the same thought is translated just as well as diverse sentences composed of entirely different words, provided these words have the same connection between them. (Bergson 1992: 121)

The feeling or intensity at the origin of thought is drawn from the duration or milieu in which thought takes place. From this perspective, it could be said that not only mathematical concepts betray movements, even they are impregnated with a certain sense of time: giving credence to the idea that chaos theory and postmodernity have something in common with the sensibilities of the 1960s. The formation of any mode of thought or being takes place within a sense of movement which is manifest and transformed as it is actualized. Furthermore, the distinction between actual form and virtual idea provides the foundation for conceiving of homologous movements in thought. Since thought is expressed in terms of a virtual 'disposition' which can be actualized in any image whatever, music and literature, the plastic arts and cinema, even philosophy and science, can, in this sense, express the same intensive movements. Bergson also describes this transcendence of movement as the basis of sense in language:

> The truth is that above the word and above the sentence there is something much more simple than a sentence or even a word: the meaning, which is less a thing thought than a movement of thought, less a movement than a direction. (Bergson 1992: 121)

As the sense of a melody is that which can only be heard, the 'meaning' of language is that given in language which can only be thought. It is the expression and apprehension of sense which is irreducible to signification, while the domain of sense subsists in the absolute duration of substance. This 'substantial duration', as Bergson terms it, consists of a virtual multiplicity of movements or 'tendencies' which enfold time or memory into the absolute continuity of life. This pure multiplicity is nowhere to be found in the Library of Babel, it is expressed solely in the enduring sensibilities of the living, for there is nowhere else for the infinitive of thought to be found.

Thought's infinitive emerges at every point where the 'pure intellect' discovers its limit and ground. This limit is not, however, simply the undecidable, the chaotic, the clinamen, the indiscernible, the unnameable, or any of the other myriad metaphors given to the 'beyond' which, as Gödel revealed, the intellect constructs from within. (Maybe it is worth noting, although at the risk of appearing overly dramatic, that those thinkers who unmasked the undecidable but were equally denied an avenue for expression – Cantor, Turing, Post and Gödel – each took their own life.) As Bergson insists, the discovery of the intellect together with its limitations offers nothing other than the potential for an alternative. As the limit of thought is time, it is time itself which must be enfolded within thought.

CHAPTER 2

Evolution Past and Present

continuity and transformation

Following the publication of Darwin's *Origin of Species*, the general principle of evolution has become widely accepted as being beyond dispute. However, while the theory of evolution has certainly changed the way in which we view life, there has been little or no change in our thought on life itself. Science and religion remain as divided as they were in Darwin's day. Broadly speaking, science consider any idea of 'creation' to be fanciful as well as purposeless, citing random variation as the only source of material change. From the Christian perspective, scientific materialism ignores the creation of 'life' itself – a quality generally considered to transcend material form and ultimately to derive from the 'creator'.

The scientific and the theological perspectives continue the dualism of materialism and idealism that has divided Western thought throughout its history. The division between science and the Church is more than epistemological, for it has become increasingly actualized socially in recent years. In this sense, scientific materialism complements the ongoing materialization that is transforming the nature of both society and the subject. In response to what an increasing number conceive to be the spiritual vacuum of scientific materialism, the decline in religious faith appears to have reversed. 'Creationism' now has a statistically higher following in the United States than Darwin. If anything, the evolution debate is only pushing science and the Church further apart and is no closer to being resolved.

In recent years, 'life' has become an increasingly vacuous but, at the same time, extremely influential term. From the medical point of view, for instance, life has become synonymous with survival and longevity. However, as illustrated by the fact that in a laboratory an animal is effectively indistinguishable from an inert chemical compound, science is incapable of differentiating between the material and the living. With the advance of modern science, the status of human life has become hard to define. The overall aim of medicine is simply to extend the mechanical functioning of the body. In this regard, life-support systems have confused the boundaries between the living and the dead. With the arrival of the likes of abortion and genetic manipulation, the medical sciences have further raised ethical questions concerning the 'nature' of life itself.

With respect to the numerous ethical crises that have resulted from advances in medicine and genetics, both theology and science are clearly incapable of providing adequate solutions. The opposition between material existence and life reappears in the growing conflict between those who demand power over their material lives and those who wish to impose a 'life-sentence' on everyone. While our knowledge of material order may have advanced in leaps and bounds since Darwin's time, our understanding of 'life' itself has only regressed if it has moved at all. It is essential, for this reason, that we find a position outside of science that is beyond 'good and evil' and does not conflict with the possibilities that science offers.

From the religious perspective, ideas such as God and life make up for the shortcomings of scientific materialism. Life, in this sense, is equivalent to the mysterious 'vital' force that animates the mortal body, giving it the freedom to think and act. God is seen to have animated the universe, being the 'prime mover' who created life and set the whole process of existence in motion. Although religion, as Bergson says of vitalism, 'may not explain very much', it does at least remind us that we are ignorant of what motivates life, the universe and change (Bergson 1983: 42). On the other hand, as Bergson further points out, modern science ignores our ignorance altogether. Replacing God and creation with the big bang, for instance, simply gives another name to the prime mover. To say the universe is fifteen billion years old is only to deny the fact that science is as much incapable of determining the beginning of time and causality as religion.

Just as the big bang is a substitute for the creator, ideas such as chance and chaos have now replaced 'creation'. While there is little doubt about the validity of Darwin's theory, the series of changes and branches do not so much represent the evolutionary process but its history. For the same reason that the 'indivisibility' of life is incontestable, the evolutionary process must be seen to be absolutely continuous. As change can only be represented as a set of discrete steps, the evolutionary process is itself beyond representation. Scientific theory, however, completely overlooks the fact that *living* organisms evolve.

'Ignorance' and the limits of representation reappear in the idea of chance, or random mutation, which serves as the sole motor of evolutionary change. An almost universally accepted term, chance has as much epistemological validity as Leibniz's 'infinitesimal'. Unrepresentable in itself, chance occurs only between steps in the infinitely divisible continuity of evolutionary history. Nevertheless, as the force behind genetic mutation, chance is now considered to have produced every facet of biological life. While genetic variation is certainly fundamental to the sexual reproduction of virtually all species, 'mutation' has never been shown to have produced anything but 'mistakes'. If anything, genetic variation is one of the primary means by which species preserve their form rather than transform. By utilizing variation in order to survive, for instance, certain strains of bacteria have remained unchanged throughout the duration of evolutionary history. Furthermore, there is absolutely no evidence of the huge number of 'failures' statistics demands.

Despite the inconsistencies, contemporary neo-Darwinists take chance to be given, producing elaborate 'proofs' that there has been enough random mutation to produce any 'possible' form. When chance is used to account for forms that have evolved independently on numerous occasions, such as with the eye, the statistics drift off into stupidity. If everything, including human sexual difference, originates from the random mutation of genes, then there are an awful lot of lucky people living in the Castro valley. In all, chance now has as much empirical evidence and dogmatic adherents as religious faith.

The first step in resolving the evolution–creation debate lies in recognizing that it is the *problem* itself that is false. Chance and creation are nothing more than synonyms for the limits of representation. Secondly, from the point of view of continuity, life, creation and material existence are inseparable from one another. Accordingly, as Spinoza argues, the prime mover is immanent to substance, making change *cause of itself*. In contrast to the rather feeble idea that the elephant existed as a possibility in the genes of an amoeba, 'life' must be seen as a force that gives rise to differences that might never have been. Although scientists may smirk at the idea the nature of life may be beyond our understanding, the union of life and force is certainly more valid, 'scientifically' and intuitively, than the petty nihilism currently accompanying Darwinian theory which is more fitting of emotionally isolated teenage boys than of conscious existence.

Once chance is removed from the evolutionary equation, we need no longer reduce life to a series of possible failures. The relations that compose the organic environment, moreover, are far more complex and intricate than those represented by the struggle for survival. While survival is certainly a factor in the composition of the environment, fitness alone in no way accounts for the relations between individual organisms, the structure of their organs and the nature of their instincts and actions. Continuity demands that we recognize material life itself to be a *formative* power where change does not happen by chance but, as Bergson argues, in reply to problems and potentials manifest in the changing environment (Bergson 1983: 58). Similarly, being inseparable from the living, life need no longer be thought of as some indifferent force to be preserved at all costs, but rather a potential that has no existence other than in the differences embodying it.

In *Creative Evolution* Bergson approaches evolution as a *living* process. Accepting the material reality we perceive exists, Bergson finds no reason to refute Darwin's account of evolution as the continued variation of material composition. Following Darwin, the emergence of form must be regarded as the result of the evolutionary process itself. However, Bergson argues that Darwinism fails to account for evolution as a *continuous* process. In this respect, Bergson's interpretation of Darwinism replicates his reading of Zeno: in reducing evolution to a discrete series of material variations or genetic mutations both Darwinism and neo-Darwinism describe the *trajectory*, or history, of evolution, but in so doing they negate a priori the continuity of evolution as a *living* process.

In an account of his own philosophical evolution, Bergson recalls that it was through his initial interest in evolutionary theory that he became aware of the significance of the continuity of *lived* time:

I was indeed very much struck to see how real time, which plays the leading part in any philosophy of evolution, eludes mathematical treatment. Its essence being to flow, not one of its parts is still there when another part comes along. Superposition of one part on another with measurement in view is therefore impossible, unimaginable, inconceivable. (Bergson 1992: 12)

The simple and undeniable fact of 'lived' time is that it cannot 'pass', it cannot be divided and, for that reason, it cannot be represented. Other than as represented in an imaginary space, it can never be said of life that it ever 'was': life can only be thought in the infinitive. Extrapolating from this, Bergson contends that the 'life' of the evolutionary process must also be regarded as an absolute continuum. If development, life and evolution are considered as equally continuous, then in the duration of evolution there is no 'moment' in which a genetic state can be isolated from all the others, that the germ can be separated from the cytoplasm, DNA from proteins, cells from organism, or organism from environment and so on. For this reason, Bergson declares that the evolutionary process itself is synonymous with substantial becoming or 'duration'.

In *Creative Evolution* Bergson analyses the principal accounts of evolution from both the epistemological and biological perspectives. This is undertaken in order to expose the implicit contradiction between the scientific method and the nature of enduring processes. In relying on some fundamental unit from which to reconstruct the evolutionary process, both neo-Darwinism and neo-Lamarckism, for example, commit a form of epistemological murder. The assumption that individual organisms can be conceived in isolation, or that genetic configurations represent a given 'state', contrasts with the continuity that is 'lived'. If the interaction between organism and environment, as well as between the germ and soma, is continuous or enduring then individuality 'admits of any number of degrees' while the concept of a unit can only be 'provisionally final' (Bergson 1983: 12, 154). Given that an investigation into evolutionary processes must begin with the analysis of discrete data, Bergson contends that the interpretation of scientific data must be *complemented* by a philosophical account of process.

In the first chapter of *Creative Evolution* Bergson enacts this dual method in a sustained analysis of the problem of homology. Each of the then current theories of evolution is tested for its ability to account for the emergence of isomorphic forms across distinct phylogenetic lines:

> In thus submitting the various present forms of evolutionism to a common test, in showing that they all strike against the same insurmountable difficulty, we have in no wise the intention of rejecting them altogether. On the contrary, each of them, being supported by a considerable number of facts, must be true in its way. Each of them must correspond to a certain aspect of the process of evolution. Perhaps it is necessary that a theory should restrict itself exclusively to a particular point of view, in order to remain scientific, *i.e.* to give a precise direction to researches into detail. But the reality of which each of these theories takes a partial view must transcend them all. And this reality is the special object of philosophy . . . (Bergson 1983: 84)

During this discussion, Bergson reveals a very deep understanding of the various evolutionary theories which were then in the air. As the above quotation suggests, none are rejected *tout court*. First, Bergson agrees with the neo-Darwinian view that all roads in development lead back to the germ-plasm. However, he argues that the simple formula of random genetic variation and natural selection fails adequately to account for the homologous emergence and continuous function of complex organs. Second, Bergson argues that *if* some somatic changes during development or responses to environmental conditions could be shown to influence the germ-line, then the assumed 'passivity' of variation is placed in question. He leaves this as an open question, validated by the limitations of neo-Darwinism. Third, he suggests that as any change in a complex organic structure must effect changes throughout the whole in order for it to continue to function, then variation should equally be attributed to the varied correlation of genes rather than, say, to individual genes themselves. Fourth, as functions are equally correlated with the environment then adaptation should not be reduced to the individual organism but to the environment itself. That is, adaptation must be regarded as *coevolutionary*. Finally, the prevalence of homologies transcending independent phyla suggests the existence of evolutionary movements immanent to, and traversing, the environment as a whole. In order to account for this, Bergson proposes the concept of the tendency, which he likens to 'problems' immanent to the evolutionary process. Such tendencies transcend the limits of isolated genes and independent organisms and account for the 'logical affiliation' between homologous forms.

The aim of what follows will be to examine this Bergsonian formula in detail and in relation to a number of contemporary concepts in evolutionary theory. The result will be to show that Bergson offers a complex and comprehensive theory of evolution. The concept of the tendency offers a broad platform from which to unite paleontology with a general theory of morphogenesis. As a means of demonstrating this, Bergson's concept will be elaborated alongside Pierre-Paul Grassé's (1977) paleontological mapping of broad evolutionary movements, Brian Goodwin's (1984) field theory, and D'Arcy Thompson (1992) and Alan Turing's (1992) theories of morphogenesis. Also, positive replies to Bergson's challenge to show that somatic changes can influence the germ-line, can be found in Mae-Wan Ho's (1984) idea of the phenocopy and Edward Steele *et al.*'s (1998) discovery of evidence that acquired immunities leave an adaptive 'signature' on the chromosomal DNA. Theoretically, the idea of a fluid genome is comparable to Georg Kampis's (1991) concept of 'component systems'. Finally, the combined conceptions of duration and tendency provide a means of surmounting the Lamarck–Darwin opposition by maintaining the continuity of the germ-line but implicating it in the continuous transformation of morphological fields expressed by the continuous processes of emergence and coevolution.

Considering that neo-Darwinism has almost completely dominated evolutionary science since the publication of *Creative Evolution*, Bergson's interpretation of evolution can be regarded as contemporary. Of all the sciences, none is more dominated by dogmatic orthodoxy than neo-Darwinism. Weismann's barrier appears to apply to evolutionary theory as much as it does to the organisms it studies: there have been virtually no changes to the central tenets of natural selection and random variation in spite of the limited perspective they offer of the evolutionary process and the numerous more congruous alternatives that have arisen this century. The most outspoken adherent of dogmatic neo-Darwinism of late has been Daniel Dennett. In his recent *Darwin's Dangerous Idea* Dennett gives an indication of the strength of his faith in the science:

> The fundamental core of contemporary Darwinism, the theory of DNA-based reproduction and evolution, is now beyond dispute among scientists. It demonstrates its power every day, contributing crucially to the explanation of planet-sized facts of geology and meteorology, through middle-sized facts of ecology and agronomy, down to the latest microscopic facts of genetic engineering. It unifies all of biology and the history of our planet into a single grand story. (Dennett 1995: 20)

The almost exclusive role played by DNA in reproduction, ontogeny and phyletic continuity may be incontestable but to suggest that neo-Darwinism is 'beyond dispute' among scientists is simply rhetoric. Dennett's stance invites comparison with Russell's fated claim that 'Cantor's continuum is free from contradictions.' Replicating this rhetorical stance, Dennett reproduces Russell's duality of 'mysticism and logic', neatly dividing the philosophy of evolution into what he terms legitimate scientific 'cranes' and foundationless 'skyhooks'. Dennett contends that Darwinism and the scientific disciplines that support it represent fundamental 'cranes' of knowledge upon which an evolutionary 'theory of everything' can be engineered. Anything which cannot be directly verified by scientific analysis or experiment is, according to Dennett, not only inadmissible in the evolutionary debate but invariably a skyhook upon which we pin our hopes that Darwin's 'dangerous idea' might be false. For this reason, any encounter with Dennett from the point of view of Bergsonism amounts to something of a replay of the Russell–Bergson debate.

In the process of demonstrating Bergson's importance to evolutionary theory, any association between Bergson and vitalism will be dispelled. Ironically, Bergson was openly critical of the vitalism which is now associated with his name. He was careful not to associate himself directly with vitalists such as Driesch, who proposed the existence of some organismic entelechy 'superposed on mechanism' (Bergson 1983: 42n). 'Vitalism', as Bergson saw it, was nothing but a sign of the fact that we are inescapably immersed in the continuity of process:

> We shall not reproach [vitalism], as is ordinarily done, with replying to the question by the question itself: the 'vital principle' may indeed not explain very much, but it is at least a sort of label affixed to our ignorance, so as to remind us of this occasionally, while mechanism invites us to ignore that ignorance. (Bergson 1983: 42)

In this respect, it is the 'vital' fact that living processes are continuous which will be shown to conflict with Dennett's ultra-mechanistic account of evolution and to expose the ignorance he invites us to ignore. When confronted by the same questions of the 'whole' which troubled the logical origins of set theory, the paradoxical limitations of Dennett's atomistic and mechanistic ontology are exposed, and the importance of the questions of duration and continuity highlighted. The random, with which neo-Darwinism fills the gaps in mechanistic thought, gives way in the end to movement, and it is in terms of movement, of the *evolving* and not the *evolved*, that we must approach evolution as a living process.

BEYOND NEO-DARWINISM

Creative Evolution was written soon after the appearance of neo-Darwinism, which emerged from the synthesis of the Darwinian principles of natural selection and random mutation with Weismann's then recent distinction between the germ and the soma. Weismann pointed out that only the information contained in the 'germ', or what we now know as DNA, is transmitted from one generation to the next. Further to this, he maintained that characteristics acquired during development have no effect on the germ. What has now become known as Weismann's 'barrier' restricts mutation purely to the genetic code, precluding any influence of organismic development or change in the soma on the evolutionary process. The 'strong' neo-Darwinian position which dominates to this day considers ontogeny to be completely genetically encoded and phylogenetic transformation to arise solely through the combined forces of genetic mutation and natural selection. Kim Sterelny examplifies the neo-Darwinian faith in the selective power of natural selection in a review of Richard Dawkins' *The Blind Watchmaker*. Sterelny, when questioning Dawkins' belief in the ability of natural selection to tell the difference between two 'protostick insects' where one looks 5 per cent like a stick and another 4 per cent, writes: 'Still, I do think this objection is something of a quibble because essentially I agree that natural selection is the only possible explanation of complex adaptation. So something like Dawkin's stories *have got to be right*' (Sterelny 1988: 424; my emphasis). This is hardly science and it certainly does not have to be the case. Rejecting the blind acceptance of the powers of chance while, at the same time, maintaining Weismann's distinction between the germ and soma, Bergson points out that genetic variation is neither random nor unaffected by development:

> The neo-Darwinians are probably right, we believe, when they teach that the essential causes of variation are the differences inherent in the germ borne by the individual, and not the experiences or behavior of the individual in the course of his career. Where we fail to follow these biologists is in regarding the differences inherent in the germ as purely accidental and individual. (Bergson 1983: 85)

The prevalence of homologous forms, where similar structures, not governed by the same genes, appear across distinct evolutionary phyla, calls into question the assumption that genetic mutation is essentially random. Without the fantastic power of chance, natural selection is unable to offer a viable account of homology, as from the neo-Darwinian perspective the two terms are essentially synonymous.

In addressing the problem of homology Bergson repeatedly returns to Darwin's discussion of the evolution of the eye. In *The Origin of Species*, Darwin argues that even an organ as complex as the eye has evolved simply from the combined effects of variation and selection. He contends that the increased complexity of the eye must have resulted from certain variations giving the organism an advantage in the struggle for survival and nothing more. As mutation and selection must account for all forms, Darwin challenges that 'If it could be demonstrated that any complex organ existed, which could not possibly have been formed by numerous, successive, slight modifications, my theory would absolutely breakdown' (Darwin 1993: 232).

Bergson's discussion focuses on the problem of the eye, for its evolution involves a number of separate issues. First, it is a prime example of homology. Bergson cites the fact that the eye has evolved independently in molluscs and vertebrates as evidence that the appearance of the organ is not a complete fluke. Although, as Darwinism necessitates, all species are genetically related, Darwin's assumption that morphology can be reduced to heredity is complicated by the fact that eyes have appeared independently across what is now believed to be at least 40 phylogenetically distinct species (Goodwin 1997: 148). Second, Bergson argues that since the organ must continue to function throughout variation, genetic mutations must be in some way coordinated. The emergence of a lens, for example, requires changes in the organ as a whole if it is to continue to function. Third, if transformation is the result of an accumulation of slight variations, then the ability for natural selection to account for continuity is placed in question. Variations in the structure and function of the eye would have to be so insensible for it to continue to work that it is highly doubtful that natural selection could play its part. In the end, Bergson accepts Darwin's claim that evolution is a process of 'numerous, successive slight modifications' but he disputes both the idea that these are purely accidental and that natural selection can adequately account for their accumulation.

In *Darwin's Dangerous Idea*, Dennett attempts to demonstrate that neo-Darwinism explains the *whole* of evolution and consequently takes Darwin's challenge literally as a do or die threat. Accordingly, he insists that the 'numerous slight modifications' through which change is incremented *must* be provided by random mutation and accumulated by natural selection. However, as there is no way of verifying experimentally if natural selection can act as a generator of form, nor any way of proving that the enormous number of mutations necessary to produce so many right combinations has occurred, Dennett translates the basic principles of Darwinism, variation and selection, into purely theoretical concepts. First, variation and mutation are conceived as expressions of the combinatory space of 'genetic possibility'. Put simply, any finite number of specific genetic states presents a potential domain of possible combinations. Second, 'survival' is translated into 'probability'. If an organism is better adapted its probability of survival will increase. Taken together, Dennett argues that if variation produces enough possibilities then the appropriate solution will probably appear, and if similar environments and similar environmental problems exist, then homology will be a likely event.

Dennett believes that rather than testing the theory of natural selection, homology is proof that natural selection determines optimum levels of fitness within the environment which transcend individuals and species. The struggle between individual organisms creates what Dennett calls a 'design space' and the nature of engineering determines certain 'forced moves'. With the emergence of locomotion and the potential for sight that light provides, vision itself appears as a possibility in evolutionary design space. As this potential applies to any moving organism, the independent evolution of vision is plausible:

We know that eyes have evolved independently many times, but vision is certainly not a necessity on Earth, since plants get along fine without it. A strong case can be made, however, that *if* an organism is going to further its metabolic projects by locomoting, and *if* the medium in which the locomoting takes place is transparent or translucent and amply supplied by ambient light, then *since* locomoting *works much better* (at furthering self-protective, metabolic, and reproductive aims) if the mover is guided by information about distal objects, and *since* such information can be garnered in a high-fidelity, low-cost fashion by vision, vision is a very good bet. So we should not be surprised to find that locomoting organisms on other planets (with transparent atmospheres) had eyes. Eyes are an obviously good solution to a very general problem that would often be encountered by moving metabolizers. (Dennett 1995: 128)

Bergson himself also argues that sight is the solution to a 'problem'. However, he considers the neo-Darwinian presumption that selection is the only active force in the production of form to inevitably accord an element of finality to the 'natural'. Since for the neo-Darwinist the genetic basis to any form can only be attributed to blind variation, homology must be explained by similarity on the level of 'fitness'. But, as Bergson points out, one fundamental problem with this is that material form and fitness, 'organ and function, are terms of different nature' (Bergson 1983: 62). In neo-Darwinism 'adaptation' has no direct relation to material variation, it arises through natural selection where the external relations between competing individuals determine scales of fitness. Bergson points out that neo-Darwinism reproduces a variation of the Aristotelian 'formal' cause by considering material variations to be 'adapted' when they coincide with an external form (Bergson 1983: 57). In the same manner that any liquid 'adapts' its shape to that of the container when it is poured into a glass, neo-Darwinism presupposes that variation is passive and that matter is essentially inert. Bergson considers science in general to reduce process solely to the transformation of material composition, and when this is transposed onto the problem of evolution it has the effect of eliding any 'activity' on the part of the organism. As he writes:

> The gradual complication of a form which is better and better adapted to the mould of outward circumstances is one thing, the increasingly complex structure of an instrument which derives more and more advantage from these circumstances is another. In the former case, the matter merely receives an imprint; in the second, it reacts positively, it solves a problem. Obviously it is this second sense of the word 'adapt' that is used when one says that the eye has become better and better adapted to the influence of light. But one passes more or less unconsciously from this sense to the other, and a purely mechanistic biology will strive to make the *passive* adaptation of an inert matter, which submits to the influence of the environment, mean the same as the *active* adaptation of an organism which derives from this influence an advantage it can appropriate. (Bergson 1983: 70)

The elision of any active influence on the part of the organism results from the fact that neo-Darwinism perceives the substance of evolution as science perceives matter in general. However, the presumption that matter is inert and that changes in function are due solely to the selective and cumulative effects of natural selection leads to a number of anomalies in the neo-Darwinian theory of adaptation and requires adherence to numerous unverifiable presuppositions.

Bergson points out that throughout its evolution the eye must have proceeded through such an infinitesimally slight series of adjustments as to make the viability of natural selection highly improbable. As Darwin himself notes, for an organ as complex as the eye to continue to function throughout its evolution the variations it passes through would have to be 'insensible' (Darwin 1993: 228). Natural selection would have to be almost infinitely accurate in order to account for the enormous number of tiny variations and additions to the neuronal, musculature and nervous systems that need to be correlated with the appearance of new componentry, and the equally numerous number of variations which must be accumulated before a new component emerges. Further to this, during the passage from the structure of the earliest pigment spot to the eye of the vertebrates, the eye must not only continue to function but also improve to such a degree as to offer a selective advantage. There is absolutely no paleontological evidence of the immense number of possible failures necessary to make such an assumption 'probable'; neither is the selective power of natural selection verifiable in any way. Natural selection can only be maintained as the sole factor in adaptation as a matter of faith.

Dennett, however, takes the passivity of variation as a given and is adamant that natural selection is the *only* factor in adaptation. In order to account for the adaptation of all forms he describes variation as giving rise to a 'field of possibilities' (Dennett 1995: 108–12). Evolutionary possibility is conceived as the genetic potential of the sum of configurations contained in the combinations of the basic elements of the DNA. Dennett considers this possible space to be analogous to Borges' metaphor of a 'universal library', which contains 'all possible books' constructed from all possible combinations of the alphabet. Given the elements of DNA, it is proposed that it is equally possible to conceive of a 'Library of Mendel' which contains the infinite collection of all possible genetic configurations. From this perspective, all of the genetic states corresponding to variations of the structure of the eye subsist in 'genetic space' as a sort of pool of evolutionary potential. Genetic variations that are actualized through reproduction draw from this potential. Dennett argues that given enough time it is probable that the genetic configuration of a more efficient structure will eventually be selected. As natural selection preserves variations which increase fitness, the increased complexity of the eye becomes, according to Dennett, a 'probability'. As the potential configurations of the basic elements of the DNA contain all possible evolutionary forms, Dennett regards this combination of genetic possibility and probability to account for evolution as a whole.

Although viewing the evolutionary process as a combination of possibility and probability is, as Bergson would say, 'intelligible', it appears somewhat facile when applied to actuality. For example, from this perspective, the extraordinary fact that the marsupial and placental mammals have evolved in parallel since they were separated some 65 million years ago, amounts to nothing more than the realization of 'practical possibilities'. Although they share the same parental form, since the time of separation the principal representatives of the placental mammals, such as wolves, cats, squirrels, anteaters, moles and mice have evolved independently in marsupial form. To infer from this that a 'mouse' is a 'probability' does not really amount to saying very much. As Bergson suggests, that two people walking at random should eventually cross paths is one thing, but that they should have both followed the exact same route is another (Bergson 1983: 57). Even if one accepts the dubious idea that the form of 'mouse' exists somewhere in a space of genetic possibilities, to suggest that it is 'probable' that the same form will be hit upon in two parallel phyla and that the same probability is repeated with the wolf and the anteater and so on is nothing more than word-play. For one, the only evidence we have are the actual species themselves, there is no paleontological record of the potentially infinite series of 'possibilities' which would have to have been actualized in order for the 'probabilities' to emerge. As the following quotation attests, Dennett's conception of possibility expresses nothing more than the potential of language:

With hindsight, we can say that tigers were in fact possible all along, if distant and extremely improbable. One of the virtues of this way of thinking of possibility is that it joins forces with probability, thus permitting us to trade in flat all-or-nothing claims about possibility for claims about relative distance . . . As we saw in our exploration of the Library of Babel, it doesn't make much difference what our verdict is about whether it is 'possible in principle' to find some particular volume in that Vast space. What matters is what is practically possible. (Dennett 1995: 119)

It is here that the principle of 'possibility' becomes clearly absurd. There is no doubt that everything that will be written in the English language is contained in the infinite combinations of the letters of the alphabet, but this tells us very little about either meaning or composition. To say that 'tigers' were a possibility before they evolved is as meaningful as stating that someday the world will be populated by Boblets and Spings.

Not only is Dennett's idea of probability meaningless in this regard, but his conception of possibility hides some fairly extravagant epistemological assumptions. Bergson provides a powerful critique of the idea of possibility in his essay 'The Possible and the Real'. In this text he argues that it is only 'with hindsight' that the 'possible' can be said to come into existence. For example, it is only under the presupposition that tigers 'exist' that they are conceivably possible. Whereas the idea that a tiger pre-exists its actual emergence, simply overlays the abstract class through which we denote it onto its preceding history. From this perspective, as Bergson says, it is the actual which 'creates' its own possibility:

Underlying the doctrines which disregard the radical novelty of each moment of evolution there are many misunderstandings, many errors. But there is especially the idea that the possible is *less* than the real, and that, for this reason, the possibility of things precedes their existence. They would be capable of representation beforehand; they could be thought of before being realized. But it is the reverse that is true. If we leave aside closed systems, subjected to purely mathematical laws, isolable because duration does not act on them . . . we find there is more and not less in the possibility of each of the successive states than in their reality. For the possible is only the real with the addition of an act of mind which throws its image back into the past, once it has been enacted. (Bergson 1992: 99–100)

As Bergson argues, the idea of possibility is implicitly tautological: it is only once something has come into being that we can ever say that it is 'possible'. For this reason, possibility does not 'precede' actuality, it is a purely *retrospective* projection of history determined once a 'possibility' appears. Moreover, the domain of possibilities will always constitute a closed system, for possibility can only designate variations of what already is. Similarly, the belief that possibility pre-exists actuality in some empyreal design space is the ultimate expression of the spatialization of time. It is only from the point of view of the intellect that time is considered as an *extended* series of material configurations. Dennett's universal library takes this a step further, combining an essentially Epicurean ontology of a finite number of units with a purely idealist notion of eternity. The end result, the glib variation of the idea that 'anything is possible', amounts to a flat denial of Darwin's basic intuition that forms are *created*.

It is for this reason that Bergson finds no ontological difference between mechanism and finalism: both assume that ultimately 'all is given'. Finalism may understand reality as pre-existing in the form of some transcendent intellect, but equally mechanism considers that all is given in the realm of infinite possibility. As Deleuze writes in *Bergsonism*:

This is the constant theme of Bergsonism from the outset: the confusion of space and time, the assimilation of time into space, make us think that the whole is given, even if only in principle, even if only in the eyes of God. And this is the mistake that is common to mechanism and to finalism. The former assumes that everything is calculable in terms of a program: in any event, time is only there now as a screen that hides the eternal from us, or that shows us successively what a God or superhuman intelligence would see in a single glance. (Deleuze 1991: 104)

'Infinite possibility' is as much a theological notion as predetermined finality. This leaves Dennett clearly standing on the same ground as the 'creationists' he so vehemently opposes. As much as the creationists wish to attribute evolution to the mind of God, Dennett perceives that there is nothing which escapes the mind of man.

Bergson's critique of neo-Darwinism does not directly question its basic framework of natural selection and genetic variation; his primary aim is to reveal that it is not the whole story. To demonstrate this, he points out that in assuming that 'all is given' in the sum of possible material configurations, materialism inevitably stumbles upon the problem of the 'whole'. This is clearly the case with Dennett's conception of genetic 'possibility'. For in terms of the broad ontological picture, the 'universal library' metaphor runs into the problem of the 'set of all sets'. It is only from the point of view of a godlike observer that such a totality as the 'set of all sets' of possible genetic configurations can be conceived. This, as Cantor intuited at the origins of set theory, leads to the paradox of God being a member of the set or not.

In terms of sets, both instant and eternity are essentially the same. Both the elements of a set and the set of all elements can only be conceived outside of time. What this means for biology is that there is no ontological difference between conceiving of an organism as a sum of discrete genes and the idea of infinite recombinatory genetic possibility. With the former, the material body is conceived as existing in an instant; with the latter, possibility is considered to exist for all time, in eternity. The very idea of an isolated genetic state can only be conceived from the point of view of what Bergson terms 'pure perception'. The very act of determining a discrete element isolates it from temporal continuity. The ultimate objective point of view assumed in Dennett's conception of possibility takes the idea of pure perception to its infinite extreme.

In *Matter and Memory*, Bergson points out that 'pure perception', the 'coincidence of perception with the object perceived, exists in theory rather than in fact' (Bergson 1991: 66). The idea of a discrete element by nature involves it being isolated from the continuity of time, but the 'present' in which an element, or a 'unit', could be isolated is always passing, it never 'is'. From this perspective, the paradox of self-referentiality which emerges with the set of all sets applies to any 'set'. The body as the ultimate unit, or the gene as the fundamental component of evolution, can only be maintained when interaction is foreclosed. The reduction of an organism to the set of its genes, as much as the reduction of ontology to the set of possibilities, can only be considered at the expense of duration. In *Creative Evolution* Bergson reveals the neo-Darwinian conception of evolution to be conceived in the absence of life. In order to apprehend evolution as a living process it must be approached from the point of view of continuity.

ORGANISM AND MACHINE

In *Darwin's Dangerous Idea*, Dennett reduces the continuity of evolution to the dual algorithmic processes of natural selection and genetic determination. In comparing evolution to the unfolding of algorithms, he assumes that a one–one correspondence exists between mechanism and process. To articulate this, Dennett equates the genetic code in general with the Turing Machine and likens particular genetic codes to algorithms encoding specific forms. He then extends the 'Library of Mendel' metaphor to what he terms the 'Library of Toshiba' (Dennett 1995: 437). As the Turing Machine is able to encode any mechanistic process, the 'Library of Toshiba' corresponds to the infinite set of potential algorithms. Further to this, Dennett compares natural selection to a blind algorithm of selection which sifts through the space of randomly varying genetic codes selecting the fittest or the most functional:

> Here, then, is Darwin's dangerous idea: the algorithmic level *is* the level that best accounts for the speed of the antelope, the wing of the eagle, the shape of the orchid, the diversity of the species, and all the other occasions for wonder in the world of nature . . . No matter how impressive the products of an algorithm, the underlying process always consists of nothing but a set of individually mindless steps succeeding each other without the help of intelligent supervision; they are 'automatic' by definition: the workings of an automaton. (Dennett 1995: 59)

The algorithmic universe may proceed without the help of 'intelligent supervision', but it could not have arisen without it. If the 'intellect' is the 'mechanism' of thought, Darwinism presents another case of the intellect finding itself again in things. As with mechanism in general, an algorithm is, in the most basic sense as Dennett describes it, governed by 'individual steps': it is a step-by-step process. Any step-by-step process can be described by a Turing Machine, hence neo-Darwinism, as Dennett interprets it, is purely mechanical. The evolutionary process is the sum of discrete genetic codes, together with the algorithmic process of selection which determines their survival. Hence the conclusion that natural selection is a blind 'artificial intelligence'.

The Turing Machine represents a model of the reflective thought process which, in turn, defines the general principles of the work of a 'computer'. As a generalized account of any discrete state process, the Turing Machine is synonymous with what Bergson defined as the intellect. As all intellectual methods are essentially step-by-step processes, they are fundamentally incommensurate with the continuity of both the living body and the thinking mind. Because life, thought and evolution are continuous, it is impossible to wholly isolate a 'step' from the movement of the whole. A step can only be isolated once duration has 'passed'. Therefore, it is only once something has come into actuality, or a process been completed, that it can be abstracted from the whole and replayed in an algorithmic manner. Furthermore, a mechanical or algorithmic process must adopt a fundamental informational unit. The algorithmic modelling of a dynamical process will then consist in determining invariant relations between selected units: that is, the algorithm will perform a predetermined operation. As the authors of *Lamarck's Signature* point out, computer-based models of natural selection ultimately depend upon the presetting of selection criteria and the algorithmic rules for the desired result (Steele *et al.* 1998: 220). The very conception of an algorithmic process cannot proceed without this 'divine intervention'. The simple choice of unit determines a range of applicability and the negation of 'external' influences. In this sense, all algorithmic processes are 'Hamiltonian', to which complications can only be added. But in evolutionary processes, as Bergson argues, such abstraction cannot be assumed:

If science does not go to the end and isolate completely, it is for the convenience of study; it is understood that the so-called isolated system remains subject to certain external influences. Science merely leaves these alone, either because it finds them slight enough to be negligible, or because it intends to take them into account later on. It is none the less true that these influences are so many threads which bind up the system to another more extensive, and to this a third which includes both, and so on . . . (Bergson 1983: 10–11)

As Bergson points out in *Matter and Memory*, the existence of gravitational and electromagnetic fields precludes the complete isolation of any physical entity. With organic forms and the complex interdependence of species in and with the environment, the continuity of relations becomes increasingly pronounced. This compromises the idea that the evolutionary process is governed by a discrete series of mechanisms. The continuity of relations renders the algorithmic nature of the intellect incompatible with the duration of process.

Dennett presumes that the mechanism of thought and physical dynamics are the same thing. It is for this reason that in his algorithmic picture of the universe, none of the complications that arise from the continuity of both relations and time are addressed. The genetic future of an organism is assumed to be predetermined at conception and the function of each gene is considered to be isolable in time. This obviously contradicts the empirical fact that a genetic state cannot be divorced from the continuity of the organism as a living entity. The fact that the life of an organism cannot be divided means that the gene or any other unit cannot be considered in complete isolation. As Kampis and Csányi point out:

. . . a gene and a genome are *interdependent* so that the genes *mutually presuppose* each other: the functional effect of each gene makes its way through conditions set by the others, which conditions, in turn, rest upon conditions set by the gene in question. (Kampis and Csányi 1990: 388)

A *circulus vitiosus* arises from this interdependence which leads at once to the questions of time and individuation. In the continuity of development in which the genetic material is unfolded, not only do the genes mutually presuppose one another, the genome cannot be considered distinct from the cytoplasm nor from the production of proteins, cells and so on. The isolation of the genes from the soma and the soma from the environment can only take place in 'thought'. However, in the continuity of duration, the relation between genome, cytoplasm and proteins cannot be considered either in isolation or as 'successive'. Furthermore, in duration the individual cannot be isolated from its environment.

From this perspective, in terms of natural selection, if there is an algorithm determining what it is to be – say a fit rabbit – then an improvement in what makes a rabbit fit necessitates a change in the algorithm of what it means for a fox to be fit. This is the basis of the 'Red Queen' hypothesis of 'coevolution'. Here an improvement in one species is considered to amount to a loss for its neighbours in the food-chain who must themselves adapt to balance the books. Assuming that a degree of coevolution of this type is operative (as must be the case, as it would be odd to think there is an algorithm for 'fox' which could be actualized in the absence of prey) the same *circulus vitiosus* returns. That is, if increased fitness is 'successive' then there must be an originary improvement which sets the movement going. In neo-Darwinism the *circulus vitiosus* emerges where phyletic diachrony and selective synchrony merge.

It is at this point that the question of immanence must be considered, for in the continuity of duration synchrony and diachrony cannot be distinguished. For example, if there is a variation in the structure of the eye this variation must be 'correlated' in complementary changes in the entire organism in order that the organ continues to function. Added to this, Kampis proposes that the emergence of new functions in the environment means that the environment as a whole needs to adjust itself: 'We have coevolution that proceeds not because better hares require better foxes but because candidates for new species make the system "re-think" what is a hare, and what is a fox' (Kampis 1993: 136). Accordingly, the image of evolution as the transforming relations between static units must be abandoned, as in time the units are constantly changing. Further to this, as duration is absolutely continuous, processes cannot be wholly 'algorithmic' for we cannot conceive of a 'succession' of steps. The body may be regarded as a multiplicity of 'mechanisms', but only at the expense of its duration. That is, the evolutionary process as Dennett describes it is utterly devoid of 'life'. The entire text of *Darwin's Dangerous Idea* is a theoretical avoidance of the idea that evolution might apply to living organisms. The difficulty that evolution as an enduring process presents to thought is that the integration of the multiplicity of mechanisms is not itself 'mechanical'. Quite simply, the continuity of change cannot be reduced to a series of steps. For this reason, Bergson declares that 'the intellect is not made to think *evolution*' (Bergson 1983: 163). It is an undeniable fact that evolution can only take place in the *continuity of life*. In order to discern the continuity of evolution we must consider that which lies beyond the purely mechanical. Bergson describes this paradoxical relation between mechanism and continuity in terms of the function of the eye:

> The eye is composed of distinct parts, such as the sclerotic, the cornea, the retina, the crystalline lens, etc. In each of these parts the detail is infinite. The retina alone comprises three layers of nervous elements – multipolar cells, bipolar cells, visual cells – each of which has its individuality and is undoubtedly a very complicated organism: so complicated, indeed, is the retinal membrane in its intimate structure, that no simple description can give an adequate idea of it. The mechanism of the eye is, in short, composed of an infinity of mechanisms, all of extreme complexity. Yet vision is one simple fact. (Bergson 1983: 88)

Although we can decompose the eye as an apparatus into any number of component parts, with each component constituting a specific machine or function, we will never recompose 'sight' as the totality of mechanisms. Sight can only be given in the continuous integration of parts. Bergson's position here is close to that of Leibniz in the *Monadology*:

> One is obliged to admit that *perception* and what depends upon it is *inexplicable on mechanical principles*, that is, by figures and motions. In imagining that there is a machine whose construction would enable it to think, to sense, to have perception, one could conceive it enlarged while retaining the same proportions, so that one could

enter into it, just like into a windmill. Supposing this, one should, when visiting within it, find only parts pushing one another, and never anything by which to explain a perception. Thus it is in the simple substance, and not in the composite or in the machine, that one must look for perception. (Leibniz 1991: 83, section 17)

The vision which Bergson describes as 'one simple fact' is comparable to what Leibniz terms the 'simple substance'. However, since the eye cannot be divorced from the living body, and perception also includes the thing perceived, 'substance' must inevitably be extended to duration as a whole.

In *Creative Evolution* Bergson isolates that which is irreducible to the sum of constituent mechanisms in order to reverse the materialist assumptions of neo-Darwinism. In the same sense that the 'mechanism' of the eye does not explain 'sight', genetic development in itself cannot be regarded as the cause of the eye. In the continuity of duration the emergence of the organ must in some way be implicated in the simple act of vision. Bergson looks to that which is irreducible to the materiality of the organ in order to account for the appearance of homologous organs within and between phyla.

In *Creative Evolution* Bergson wishes to identify that which exists only in the duration of life in order to further account for the continuity of the evolutionary process. Science ordinarily conceives of dynamical systems as the juxtaposition of static atomic elements. However, it is common knowledge that during the lifetime of an organism its 'atomic' components are replaced numerous times without the organism disintegrating. Dynamics and process must in this sense be regarded *as* life. Ultimately, existence is no longer reducible to a solid body composed of distinct elements but to the continuity of process which maintains bodies through the flux of their components. This is the metaphysical basis upon which evolution must be thought. In the indivisible continuity of duration, no process can be reduced to the interactions of static components without transforming it into a mechanism. As Bergson writes:

That life is a kind of mechanism I cordially agree. But is it the mechanism of parts artificially isolated within the whole of the universe, or is it the mechanism of the real whole? The real whole might well be, we conceive, an indivisible continuity. (Bergson 1983: 31)

Bergson's intuition of the mechanistic as only a point of view of the whole is equally captured in Deleuze's distinction between mechanism and machinism in terms of open and closed sets (Deleuze 1986: 59). The difference between an open set and a closed set is that the latter is defined purely as an aggregate of parts, while with the former the whole and part are co-determined. Any 'part' of a mechanism must itself be considered to be a mechanism in its own right, while any change in one part implicates all the others. The continuous duration of the whole is what Deleuze terms the 'machinic'. This implication of the movement of the whole in transformation is clearly expressed in Kampis's concept of the 'component system':

[I]n component-systems the components (and their associated dynamic variables) change during the processes. The variables form a complex set, and hence in order to define and encode them we would need the result of the dynamics. This poses a problem. It is only solved if we give up the ideas of computational causality and algorithmic dynamics. Such a system cannot be described before it produces what is to be described. We can never know the next step. (Kampis 1991: 198)

Kampis and Csányi also question what are ordinarily conceived as the fundamental biological units, such as the gene and the organism employed in neo-Darwinism, as there is no guarantee that the invariant form defined by the constituent units is not itself subject to changes (Kampis and Csányi 1990). The possibility of, say, environmental changes during development, means that the properties associated with the gene cannot be adequately conceived as distinct from other entities. Similarly, if a new species is to evolve, or a new function is to emerge, then the addition of genetic material is paralleled by a change in the organism as a whole. In this sense, a component system is a dynamic system which is open to variation without disintegration. Bergson's concept of the tendency, as that which remains continuous throughout material variation, is analogous to Kampis's dynamic component system. From Bergson's perspective, however, the virtual mobility of form is enfolded in the continuity of the effect. Moreover, it is with the continuity of the effect that a component system such as the eye is actively implicated in its adaptation.

THE MECHANICS OF TRANSFORMATION

Bergson argues that for an organ such as the eye to continue to function throughout variation then any change in a part would have to be correlated genetically through the whole organism. Further to this, the fact that the structure of the eye specifies a particular function means that any transformation in the organ is equally correlated with the environment. Bergson derives a concept of correlation, nominally at least, from the examples Darwin cites in *The Origin of Species*, such as the fact that white cats with blue eyes are invariably deaf, but adds that:

> In these different examples the 'correlative' changes are only *solidary* changes (not to mention the fact that they are really *lesions*, namely, diminutions or suppressions, and not additions, which makes a great difference). But when we speak of 'correlative' changes occurring suddenly in the different parts of the eye, we use the word in an entirely new sense: this time there is a whole set of changes not only simultaneous, not only bound together by community of origin, but so coordinated that the organ keeps on performing the same simple function, and even performs it better. (Bergson 1983: 67)

For a significant transformation in the function of the eye to come about (that is, an advantageous increase in complexity) numerous simultaneous complementary mutations are required, not only in the structure of the eye but also in the optical nerve and the neuronal structure of the brain. Bergson observes that the examples of correlated mutations cited by Darwin are diminutions to fitness rather than additions. Accordingly, he argues that variation and mutation need to be distinguished. As Grassé notes, the multiple, pleiotropic, effects that have arisen from single-gene mutations have never been shown to produce anything but pathologies (Grassé 1977: 56). Considering that it is unlikely that natural selection could act on the slight variations that need to accumulate in order for a noticeable increase in function to occur, the chance of multiple coordinated mutations arising so often in history is so improbable that to adhere to it amounts to a matter of faith. It is for this reason that Goldsmith's idea of 'hopeful monsters' has been so uniformly dismissed.

Bergson does not refute Darwin's claim that evolution proceeds via the accumulation of 'numerous, successive, slight modifications'. Rather, his contention is that the evidence is against variation being random. He argues that the concept of disorder which Darwinian variation presupposes carries with it the same epistemological presuppositions as the idea of possibility. The concept of disorder relies on an idea of order with which it fails to comply (Bergson 1983: 232). That is, it is impossible to represent disorder without assuming an order to which it should have applied: a disordered room is perfectly ordered if you have no intention of tidying it up. This is clearly the case in the dualism of order and disorder implied in the dichotomous distinction between natural selection and random mutation. The neo-Darwinian insistence that there is no order at all in variation, is predicated on the *negation* of order. Selection presupposes random variation, but the random is simply that which is *not* selected. Further to this, the random introduces the *accident* of time, acting as the *deus ex machina* motivating the static atomic series of discrete mechanical states. In both cases the random simply signifies the limits of mechanism.

The homologous correlations between phyla, as well as the continued correlation of elements within the phyletic variation of the eye, point to the 'insistence' of an immanent, or what Bergson terms *vital*, order. However, such a continuous quality requires an alternative mode of reasoning:

[I]f one seeks to give 'resemblance' its exact meaning through a comparison with 'identity', it will be found, I believe, that identity is something *geometrical* and resemblance something *vital*. The first has to do with measure, the other belongs rather to the domain of art: it is often a purely aesthetic feeling which prompts the evolutionary biologist to suppose related forms between which he is the first to see a resemblance: the very design he gives these forms reveals at times the hand and especially the eye of the artist. But if the identical thus contrasts so strongly with the resembling, there might be grounds for seeking to determine, for this new category of general ideas as for the other, what makes it possible. (Bergson 1992: 58)

In contrast to accounting for homology in terms of either the geometrical principles of heredity 'identity' or to an equivalence of function, *vital* resemblances are revealed in morphological *differences*. Such relations do not simply result from the 'artistic' eye of the biologist but reveal an active morphology operative in the evolutionary process. In this respect, the evolutionary biologists to whom Bergson is referring are those who follow Goethe's aesthetic morphology rather than the neo-Darwinians.

The subject of morphology has been somewhat sidelined by neo-Darwinism's preoccupation with genetics. Although genetics can account for given forms, it leaves the question of the transmutation of form to natural selection. As we have seen, the neo-Darwinian distinction between form (natural selection) and matter (genetics) introduces numerous problems. This division has transmuted into the domain of biology itself, with the subject of morphology suffering a fate similar to neo-Lamarckism. In order to transcend this problematic division Bergson seeks to articulate a conception of morphology which does not conflict with genetic materialism.

For this reason, rather than adopt the principles of 'rational' morphology of the likes of Geoffroy St-Hilaire, where homological form is seen as the expression of invariant morphological types, Bergson conceives morphology, or what he terms 'transformism', as a productive, differentiating movement. In order to account for this productive morphology, Bergson again suggests that form must first be distinguished from function. Not only are they terms of 'different nature', he points out that it is impossible to say which comes first. Rather than compare terms of different natures, as neo-Darwinism does in tying material variation with abstract fitness, Bergson suggests 'we begin by comparing together two terms of the same nature, an organ with an organ, instead of an organ with its function' (Bergson 1983: 62). The resulting morphology:

> . . . consists above all in establishing relations of ideal kinship, and in maintaining that wherever there is this relation of, so to speak, *logical* affiliation between forms, there is also a relation of *chronological* succession between the species in which these forms are materialized. (Bergson 1983: 25)

This logical affiliation is, in part, detailed in D'Arcy Thompson's *On Growth and Form*. By comparing the forms of various species, Thompson revealed certain topological invariants transcending particular phyla. He regarded this as evidence of certain morphological constants, or 'laws of growth', structuring differentiation along particular orderly lines of development. These topological principles in turn:

> . . . not only show how real and deep-seated is the phenomenon of 'correlation', in regard to form, but it will also demonstrate the fact that a correlation which had seemed too complex for analysis or comprehension is, in many cases, capable of very simple graphic expression. (Thompson 1992: 275–6)

Thompson adopted Bergson's description of evolutionary theory as a 'science of transformations'. Bergson himself points out the association between the form assumed by 'unorganized' substances such as mixtures of oil and sugar and simple protoplasmic forms (Bergson 1983: 33). Thompson elaborates such connections in great detail, the most famous being the analogy between the shape of oil dropped in paraffin and the shape of certain jellyfish (Thompson 1992: 72–3). He produced further 'graphic' evidence of such topological forms in the morphological resemblances between various distinct species of plants and animals. These virtual topologies, Thompson argues, account for the correlation of variations and suggest that much of the transmutation of form has little to do with what neo-Darwinism regards as 'adaptation'. In keeping with these various accounts of underlying or formative topological movements, Bergson compares the actualization of specific forms to the 'solution of a problem of geometry' (Bergson 1983: 58).

René Thom has extended this idea to posit the existence of certain elementary forms or 'catastrophes' which are independent of chemical substrates and which limit the number of possible biological forms (Thom 1972).

Bergson differs from this formalist approach, however, in that he regards such topologies to be 'historical'. For example, although Thompson quotes approvingly Bergson's description of morphology as the study of 'ideal kinships' or 'logical affiliations', he distances himself from the idea that morphology is also expressed in *chronological succession*. In contrast to Bergson's claim that topological forms also evolve, Thompson writes, 'the forces that bring about the sphere, the cylinder and the ellipsoid are the same yesterday and tomorrow. A snow-crystal is the same today as when the first snows fell' (Thompson 1992: 201). The topological principles of organic form are considered to be equally invariant. Bergson, however, regards such formal qualities to be essentially created and creative. As he writes in *Creative Evolution*:

> Once more, there is no universal biological law which applies precisely and automatically to every living thing. There are only *directions* in which life throws out species in general. Each particular species, in the very act by which it is constituted, affirms its independence, follows its caprice, deviates more or less from the straight line . . . (Bergson 1983: 16)

Life, as Bergson sees it, is the production and differentiation of *tendencies*. Although tendencies are analogous to topological forms or types, they must be regarded as 'formative' rather than strictly formal. In this active sense tendencies not only govern morphology, they are continuously transforming in themselves. Moreover, any transformation of form must also be implicated in an organism's relations with the environment as a whole. In light of this, Bergson holds that evolution proceeds via the differentiation and transformation of evolutionary tendencies. Evolution produces movements, while within each broad movement speciation determines singular forms. Such tendencies are not themselves subject to the influence of natural selection, but actually produce the changes upon which natural selection asserts its power.

It is precisely this conclusion that Grassé arrives at in his description of the emergence of the mammal. According to Grassé, paleontological records reveal that the distinguishing features of mammalization, such as homeothermy and the characteristic changes in jaw structure, appeared simultaneously across all of the premammalian phyla. Similarly, the same mammalian form appears to have persisted even though populations have evolved in extremely diverse environments. Below are some of the conclusions he draws from the paleontological evidence accumulated about the development of the theriodonts: the transitional line between the reptile and mammal:

1. The evolution of the theriodonts was oriented and progressed in two directions: in a general mammalian direction; and in directions specific to each line.
2. Mammalian characters are not the same in all the theriodont lines, nor are they expressed in equal or identical manner in all. Each line imposes, to a greater or lesser extent, its distinctive style.
3. The variations undergone by the theriodont reptiles accumulate with the passing of time (this idea is expressed by the term 'tend to').
4. The variations are complementary and when they appear they induce coordinated variations, such as the development of the dentary with concomitant transformation of the jaw muscles . . . (Grassé 1977: 49)

As Grassé forcefully argues in the *Evolution of Living Organisms*, if we focus on the paleontological records of the early mammals what we are presented with is the continuous, coordinated and progressive emergence of a general mammalian form. Within this movement we find a multiplicity of correlated changes including the parallel transformation of all sense organs, the transition from incubation to gestation and the emergence of homeothermal body heat regulation. Paleontological evidence points to a movement of change which is incomprehensible as an accumulation of random variations. The number of coordinated mutations that would have to be allowed in order to explain such a movement in genetic terms, simply verifies the fact that it is only intelligible as a movement or a tendency. Similarly, natural selection is unable to account for the fact that the same changes have arisen across distinct species and in starkly varying climatic and environmental conditions. Furthermore, natural selection is unable to account for the extraordinary fact that the same mammalian form traverses the marsupial and placental species.

As Grassé points out, neo-Darwinian theory 'holds true so long as it does not have to face reality, whose complexity is overwhelming' (Grassé 1977: 114). This is not to reject Darwin's insight but simply to point out that there is more to the evolutionary process than the sum of chance and necessity. As Bergson intuited, and Grassé graphically demonstrates, the paleontological evidence points to the existence of formative tendencies governing speciation and transformation. Bergson's aim, in *Creative Evolution*, is to reveal that the seemingly 'vague' idea of the tendency is a means of bringing a greater precision to evolutionary theory and philosophy in general. As Grassé endeavours to show, there is a virtual 'something' orienting the emergence and development of broad evolutionary movements such as that of the mammal. But such qualities cannot be represented, for they constitute process itself. Grassé presents the 'vital' morphological resemblances within and between emergent forms to give a sense of evolution as a 'formative' process. His work is exemplary of what Bergson termed a *'mechanics of transformation'* (Bergson 1983: 32). Bergson compares this 'mechanics' to a sort of 'temporal' calculus where material modes are the equivalent of 'differentials'. In this case the relation between a mode and a tendency 'would be like passing from the function to its derivative, from the equation of the curve (i.e. the law of the continuous movement by which the curve is generated) to the equation of the tangent giving its instantaneous direction' (Bergson 1983: 32). The difference between a tendency and a differential equation is that the former is not 'written in advance'. The tendency is defined as an open and varying continuity of change which cannot be reduced to the sum of the changes that actualize it. As Bergson conceives it, tendencies are manifest in differential relations within the environment. Such relations give rise to an immanent 'potential' for change. This potential has no determinate quality as regards form, rather it poses a general 'problem' which admits of any number of solutions. Furthermore, with the emergence of any 'solution' new parameters are introduced into the environment which transform the given relation and create further potentials. The mammal, for example, can be regarded as a general solution to the problems of mobility and independence. With the mammalian form, homeothermy offers freedom to survive in varying climates, musculature and skeletal changes progress towards increased mobility and gestation allows for the young to accompany their parents, and so on. With birds we find the general solution to the 'potential' for flight offered by the air. In this sense, Bergson 'inverts' the neo-Darwinian definition of adaptation. Species present 'active' responses to broad potentials which arrive with environmental changes. Such potentials or tendencies are immanent to the movement of change.

From this perspective all emergent forms must be considered a 'success' rather than a potential failure (Bergson 1983: 129). Each form is a specific response to the demands of the environment. Accordingly, different species and functions cannot be compared in terms of quantitative levels of fitness. It is absurd to suggest that a bird is 'better' at flying than a bat, for a bat's mode of flight is specific to its needs. For this reason, natural selection does not have any role to play in the 'production' of form. Evolutionary movements produce the forms given to selection and natural selection operates on the diseased, lame, malnourished and the 'mutated'.

As with Darwin, Bergson considers speciation to be governed by an instinct for survival. However, rather than serving as a motor of transformation, Bergson contends that survival introduces an inertia into the movement of change. Once they appear, 'each species behaves as if the general movement of life stopped at it instead of passing through it. It thinks only of itself, it lives only for itself' (Bergson 1983: 255). The stability of form is one of the most prominent characteristics of evolution. The primordial bacteria, for example, from which life in general has evolved, have remained virtually unchanged since their appearance. This contrasts with the massive potential for mutation manifest in bacterial reproduction. For this reason, Grassé proposes that genetic variation serves as a form of phyletic 'resistance'. He points out that variation is the means by which bacteria have managed to survive in the same form. Genetic variation, from this perspective, appears to fluctuate around a median position as a means of resisting change (Grassé 1977: 87). Moreover, as Bergson points out, the reproductive process in plants and animals is virtually the same despite the fact they have endured millions of years of separation (Bergson 1983: 59). It is feasible that the massive genetic overproduction characteristic of the reproductive process in nearly all flora and fauna is a manifestation of the potential for 'stability in change' that genetic variation offers. Perhaps genetic variation is itself a 'tendency'.

LAMARCK AND TIME

Bergson's question to those who adhere to the Weismannian dualism of genes and soma is, '*When* can a genetic state be determined?' The neo-Darwinian answer is, 'At the moment of conception'. This leads to the idea that the future organism is encoded entirely in the genetic information. This in turn leads to the view that development can be ignored as a factor in evolution, for change can only be said to occur at the moment of conception. But, as Bergson suggests, there is no 'point' at which the genetic material can be isolated from the developing organism (Bergson 1983: 19). For this reason, it is conceivable that *some* changes in the soma could be said to affect the manner in which the genetic information is unfolded:

After having been affirmed as a dogma, the transmissibility of acquired characters has been no less dogmatically denied, for reasons drawn *a priori* from the supposed nature of germinal cells. It is well known how Weismann was led, by his hypothesis of the continuity of the germ-plasm, to regard the germinal cells – ova and spermatozoa – as almost independent of the somatic cells. Starting from this, it has been claimed, and it is still claimed by many, that the hereditary transmission of an acquired character is inconceivable. But if, perchance, experiment should show that acquired characters are transmissible, it would prove thereby that the germ-plasm is not so independent of the somatic envelope as has been contended, and the transmissibility of acquired characters would become *ipso facto* conceivable; which amounts to saying that conceivability and inconceivability have nothing to do with the case, and that experience alone must settle the matter. (Bergson 1983: 78–9)

As testament to the contemporaneity of Bergson's thought, experiment has demonstrated that certain somatic transformations are transmissible. The above quotation could practically be considered as an introduction to the recently published *Lamarck's Signature*. Here, Edward Steele *et al.* provide strong proof of the existence of a soma to germ-line feedback in the acquisition of immunities. Working from the concept of antigen-driven somatic mutation in antibody variable genes, they have produced evidence that a feedback loop from the soma to the germ-line is effected via RNA, which acts as a template for DNA synthesis via reverse transcriptase enzymes (Steele *et al.* 1998: 208). In this sense, the body's immune response to antigens leaves a 'signature' on the germ-line. This signature provides for the rapid acquisition of immunity in the infected host and is transmissible to future generations through the germ-line. The findings of *Lamarck's Signature* question both the assumption that genes remain stable throughout development and that somatic changes have no effect on the germ-line DNA.

As the authors of *Lamarck's Signature* testify, 'conceivability and inconceivability' have little to do with the study of evolution. Experiment in contemporary molecular science leaves little doubt that some influence on the germ-line DNA occurs during the life of an organism. Moreover, the evidence suggests that the soma to germ-line reverse transcription mechanism is not restricted to the immune system alone (Steele *et al.* 1998: 204). In line with this, Mae-Wan Ho has produced evidence that phenocopies, the mimicking of genetic mutations by environmentally induced transformations during epigenesis, are also transmissible. She argues that in affecting the *patterns* of gene expression, environmentally induced effects become transmissible through the cytoplasm. According to Ho, although molecular genetics is revealing that the genomic content of all organisms is capable of being read in its entirety, its primary effect is to shatter the illusion that development is simply the reading of the DNA master-code by the cellular 'slave' machinery:

On the contrary, it is the cellular machinery which imposes control over the genes. The central role of protein-protein and protein-nucleic acid interactions in the regulation of gene expression is reinforced many times over by the detailed knowledge which has recently come to light in both eukaryotic and prokaryotic systems. The classical view of an ultraconservative genome – the unmoved mover of development – is completely turned around. Not only is there no master tape to be read out automatically, but the 'tape' itself can get variously chopped, rearranged, transposed and amplified in different cells at different times. (Ho 1984: 285)

The discovery of an essentially 'fluid' genome has lead Ho to bring development back into evolutionary discourse. Organism, genome and environment must be considered as interactive, and only partially isolated factors in evolution. Environmental changes represent 'problems' to which populations of organisms respond, with the accumulation of 'phenocopies' in the cytoplasm gradually bringing about changes in the genome. From this perspective, the organism is not a static form but a dynamic system.

Through the discovery that somatic changes influence the germ-line, DNA molecular science is opening the way for a new 'synthesis' of Lamarckism and neo-Darwinism. For this reason, the dogmatic approach to the problem of evolution adopted by the likes of Dennett, only acts as a hindrance to the development of thought. As an example of this, Steele quotes from the following passage in *Darwin's Dangerous Idea* where Dennett discusses the subject of Lamarckian inheritance:

For Lamarckism to work, the information about the acquired characteristic in question would somehow have to get from the revised body part, the soma, to the eggs or sperm, the germ line. In general, such message-sending is deemed impossible – no communication channels have been discovered that could carry the traffic – but set that difficulty aside. The deeper problem lies with the nature of the information in the DNA . . . There is no point-for-point mapping between body parts and DNA parts. That is what makes it extremely unlikely – or in some cases impossible – that

any particular acquired change in a body part . . . will correspond
to any discrete change in the organism's DNA. (Dennett 1995: 322)

As the work of Ho and Steele *et al.* is testament, Dennett's first
contention is without foundation. Experimental evidence suggesting
the existence of a means of communication from the soma to the
germ-line has been available for at least three decades and continues to
be corroborated by molecular science. Moreover, although the belief
that simple changes in organismic behaviour, such as changes in habit,
are directly transmissible does not stand up to scrutiny, given the
complex interdependence of the DNA genes with one another and
with the soma, there is no reason to discount the possibility of *general*
changes to the genome arising during development. This is precisely
the position Bergson adopts in relation to Lamarckism. Although
critical of the Lamarckian idea of the transmissibility of acquired
characteristics in its bare form, Bergson does not discount the subject
of developmental change entirely:

Now, suppose that the soma can influence the germ-plasm, as those
who hold that acquired characters are transmissible. Is not the most
natural hypothesis to suppose that things happen in this second case
as in the first, and that the direct effect of the influence of the soma
is a *general* alteration of the germ-plasm? (Bergson 1983: 82)

In this sense, rather than simple changes in habit being hereditary,
Bergson considers somatic modifications to influence the general
orientation of the fluid genome. Furthermore, he considers variations
in the genome to arise 'within' the environmental demands placed on
the organism. James Baldwin, a contemporary of Bergson's, conceived
of a similar process which he termed 'organic selection'. What is now
known as the 'Baldwin Effect' attributes a degree of active selection to
the organism whereby the organism somehow accommodates itself to
conditions which are beneficial. Baldwin argued that this vague 'intelligence' of the organism to improve its relations with the environment
'prevents the incidence of natural selection' (Baldwin 1896: 447). That
which is passed on is the capacity to adapt while the continued survival

of the species gives it 'all the time necessary to get the variations required for the full instinctive performance of the function' (Baldwin 1896: 448). Although Baldwin discounted the possibility of specific changes of habit directly affecting the germ-line, he proposed that the increased ability to adapt that is transmitted gave the organism a selective advantage, allowing it to survive long enough until variations in the genome constructed an apparatus that would effect the necessary changes. As an example of this, he described the emergence of the hand as the manifestation of a general tendency to 'grasp'. Transitional forms would use whatever they had available until variations steadily contributed to the growth of a hand.

Somewhat surprisingly Dennett accepts the 'Baldwin Effect' uncritically as an example of a theoretical 'crane' (Dennett 1995: 77–80). He regards organic selection as having the effect of 'speeding up' the influence of natural selection. From Dennett's perspective, the efforts of the organism give it a more oriented trajectory through design space. However, as Ho points out, there is no connection between Baldwin's conception of ontogenetic modification and the genetic assimilation required for heredity (Ho 1984: 273). No matter how well the organism adapts to the environment, it still has to wait just as long for mutation to sift through the field of genetic possibilities. Problems such as the correlation of singular variations with the necessary general changes in both the organ and the organism still apply. In response to this, Ho revives C. H. Waddington's concept of 'canalization'. Waddington proposed that organismic responses to environmental change canalize genetic mutations in the direction of adaptation. As further testament to the relevance and complexity of his account of evolutionary development, Bergson employs this exact term to account for the specificity of function and the 'success' of organismic responses to the problems imposed upon it by the environment. Discussing the precise relation between the eye and organismic behaviour, Bergson writes: 'The vision of a living being is an *effective* vision, limited to objects on which the being can act: it is a vision that is *canalized*, and the visual apparatus simply symbolizes the work of canalyzing' (Bergson 1983: 93).

Ho's rendition of canalization distinguishes two distinct events: the intensification of response to an environmental stimulus, resulting in increases in the frequency of phenocopies, followed by the internalization of the response through genetic assimilation. Ho's interpretation of Waddington's theory is in perfect accord with Bergson's idea of canalization. Ho extends the idea of canalization to argue that 'heredity' 'does not reside exclusively in the DNA transmitted but in the entire system of interrelationships between organism and environment at all levels' (Ho 1989: 32). This is precisely how Bergson conceives of the 'tendency' as a virtual evolutionary memory. From Bergson's perspective, the fluid genome, somatic variation and the objects which relate to it in the environment are ultimately correlated in the continuity of duration by the tendency as an immanent 'problem'.

DYNAMIC SYNTHESIS

In *Creative Evolution* Bergson employs the case where two diverse species of butterfly have different wing-patterns which can be mimicked when the larva of one is submitted to the same environmental temperature as the other, as a metaphor for the general relation between cause and effect in the evolutionary process. He compares the relation between, on the one hand, the material composition of the butterfly wing and the temperature variation and, on the other, the singular pattern formations, to that between a wind-up phonograph and the melody it plays. Bergson argues that in both cases 'the quantity of the effect depends on the quantity of the cause, but the cause does not influence the quality of the effect' (Bergson 1983: 73). With the phonograph, for example, the varying amounts of tension in the spring can determine the volume and speed at which the record is played, but the sounds produced will be variations of the same melody. Bergson points out that a similar relation between cause and effect is operative with the variation of the butterflies' wing-patterns. In this case, the temperature variations affect the process or rate of pattern generation but not the basic pattern form itself. Bergson extends this metaphor to the general relation between matter and form in the evolutionary process.

The distinction between material causes and the qualitative effects of pattern formation invites comparison with Turing's theory of morphogenesis. Through studying leaf-patterns Turing discovered that homology is the rule in flora rather than the exception. Although the number of plant varieties is enormous, the distinctive kinds of leaf-pattern is rather small. Turing examined the means by which plant 'morphologies' are produced, hence the title 'morphogenesis'. He discovered that the various forms were the result of chemical patterns produced during development. These patterns were determined by reactions between plant enzymes. Although the enzymes are produced by genes, the pattern information is irreducible to the genes alone. From Bergson's perspective, although the genes are the material cause of specific pattern formations, the patterning effect differs in kind from the actual genes.

Turing's work has been furthered in a series of recent studies by Brian Goodwin. Goodwin has argued that simple morphogenetic patterns of growth can be discerned in the generation of the cellular forms of all plants and organisms. He has demonstrated that general morphogenetic patterns unfold during development which give rise to a variety of organic forms, from the shape and distribution of plant leaves, the bone structures of vertebrates to the cellular structure of the eye. As with Turing, Goodwin has demonstrated that the morpho-genetic patterns are irreducible to the genetic information in the DNA. Emerging through symmetry-breaking reactions during generation, the unfolding of the genetic material produces patterns which are not contained in the genes themselves. Further to this, Goodwin argues that patterning is not only attributable to how the local cells interact with one another, it is also influenced by the relations with neighbour-ing regions (Goodwin 1997: 49). He defines the relational structure as a whole as a morphogenetic 'field'. Goodwin has shown that in the generation of biological forms, such as the limbs of vertebrates and even the basic structure of the eye, generic types of field determine the manner in which cells are unfolded during development. Most importantly, from this perspective, a structure such as the eye cannot be reduced to the sum of its genetic parts. The field demands that the genes and the soma unfold as a relational whole. Moreover, the evolution of the eye, for example, can be regarded as a series of variations of a single morphogenetic field.

This is precisely the position that Bergson arrives at in his account of the evolution of the eye. He defines sight as a 'tendency'. The proximity of the idea of the tendency to Goodwin's concept of the field can be discerned in a further metaphor Bergson employs to describe the process of canalization. In this instance, Bergson compares the process of canalization to the movement of an invisible hand through a mass of iron filings. If the movement is stopped at any given moment the filings will be coordinated in a specific form.

> For this reason, if the arrangement of the grains is termed an 'effect' and the movement of the hand a 'cause', it may indeed be said that the whole of the effect is explained by the whole of the cause, but to parts of the cause parts of the effect will no wise correspond. (Bergson 1983: 94)

Bergson employs this metaphor to point out what he considers to be a logical anomaly in the neo-Darwinian account of adaptation. Neo-Darwinism presupposes that the material 'causes' of the eye can be traced back to a set of specific genes. The relation between the genetic material and the somatic 'effect' is assumed to be one–one: for every given gene there is a corresponding mechanism. The evolution of the eye corresponds to a discrete causal series, which can conceivably be matched with a series of additions to the eye as a coordinated set of mechanisms. The problem with this picture is that it can in no way account for the continuity of pattern or morphology in the evolution of form. As morphology results from the continuous unfolding of cells and the relations between them, morphological patterns cannot be reduced to any specific genes. From the point of view of morphogenetic fields, only the cause as a 'whole' can be compared to the effect. This whole is manifest in the continuity of development, and it is the whole which changes in the continuity of the evolutionary process.

In terms of Bergson's metaphor, the cause of the morphology of the hand, in this case, can be compared to the generic laws of generation expressed in the continuous development of the bone structure, skin, cartilage, and so on, and the specific differences encoded in the DNA. From this perspective, however, the immanent causes of morphological difference not only determine the material structure of the hand but also its function. In the process of canalization, Bergson argues, the continuity of effect is implicated in the continuity of cause. In order to correlate the concept of the tendency with the functional specificity of the organs it expresses, Bergson defines the immanent causes of evolutionary difference as virtual or general 'problems' (Bergson 1983: 58). Problems are best represented by the infinitive form of the action a function expresses. 'Sight', for example, can be expressed as the problem 'to see'. 'Grasping', Baldwin's primary example of the process of organic selection, presents the problem 'to grasp'. It is such immanent problems which give rise to homologous organs, the continuity of function in transformation, accumulate genomic variations and correlate functional specificity with the environment.

In the continuity of duration the evolutionary process must be regarded as a single continuous plane of integrated movements and functions. Within the environment each organism is immersed in a multiplicity of relations. As the evolution of an organism cannot be divorced from its immediate environment, individuality, as Bergson writes, 'admits of any number of degrees' (Bergson 1983: 12). For this reason, relations must be included in the evolutionary process. Moreover, if adaptation is regarded as 'active', relations must in some way be implicated in development.

In *Creative Evolution* Bergson argues that relations, and not individual genes or organisms, must be regarded as the primary units of the evolutionary process. From this perspective, the process of canalization traverses subject and object. The coordination of cellular development is further implicated in the relational whole as a singular 'component system' (Bergson 1983: 166). If each relation is seen as a component system, then not only the development of each organism but the organism and its ecosystem must be regarded as mutually implicated. Similarly, the multiplicity of immanent systems which constitute the environment are to varying degrees contained within each other, much like Russell's theory of logical types, except there is no discernible hierarchy and each is correlated with the whole.

During development, cells are organized to produce a specific organ, the organ is designed to produce a particular function, and the function relates to an external object. The development of the organ, in this sense, includes the nature of the external body. For this reason, Bergson argues that 'finality is external' (Bergson 1983: 41). From this perspective, Bergson's interpretation of development is proximate to neo-Lamarckism. Lamarck considered the efforts an organism makes to adjust to its environment to contribute directly to its evolution. In this case, the 'efforts' of an animal are conceived in the manner of 'intentions'. However, Bergson is critical of Lamarckism in this bare form. With an intentional action the relation between subject and object can only be regarded as successive, as the subject is considered to *react* or adapt *to* a given environment. Bergson points out that in the continuity of duration subject and object must be regarded as contemporaneous. In this sense, the organism's response must be seen as taking place within a given relation. The relation itself influences the direction of change. If we consider the relation as primary and the relational whole as a single component system, then the function of the subject becomes inseparable from the nature of its object. Subject and object can be regarded as evolving 'in tandem.'

As a concrete example of the emergence of a relational component system, Bergson describes the case of three distinct species of wasp who paralyse their prey in exactly the same way. The three species have evolved the same instinct of stinging their prey in the precise point on the nervous system where the prey will be immobilized but not killed. This procedure is carried out for the body of the prey will then be host to the wasp's larvae. By keeping the body of the prey alive, the larvae have a continuous supply of food during maturation. The larvae further maximize the effect of their parent's immobilizing sting by devouring the organs of the host, beginning with the least vital in order that its body remains alive for as long a period as possible.

In order to transcend the limited perspective neo-Darwinism offers of such a phenomena, Bergson suggests that we consider the relation not so much as between 'two organisms, but as two activities'. From the neo-Darwinian perspective this extraordinary series of complex adaptations and correlated functions is simply the result of a series of random mutations being accumulated by natural selection. The instinctual behaviour of the wasp and its larvae is attributed to the gradual accumulation of increasingly perfected genetic variations. Bergson questions this interpretation for two reasons. First, he argues that the image of an instinctual mechanism constructed by incremental units is simply a projection of the mechanistic presuppositions of the intellect which conceives the instinct in the manner of a machine. In this case, the instinctual behaviour is regarded as the accumulation of distinct atomic components, each functioning in its own right. However, any change in part would have to be correlated with the whole in order for it both to continue to function and function better. The chances of this occurring once are extreme enough, but for the instinct to evolve in parallel in three distinct species renders such an hypothesis mere conjecture. Second, Bergson questions the assumption that predator and prey evolve completely independently of one another. In order to account for the precise correlation of the wasp's intuitive knowledge with the structure of the prey's anatomy, neo-Darwinism must presuppose that the prey exists prior to the emergence of its predator's instinct. However, there is no evidence that the two species did not evolve in tandem. Moreover, if natural selection is to account for this case it must be used 'selectively' as it would be inconsistent not to assume the prey would not have mutated some form of defence. In this sense, the correlation of the prey's anatomy with the predator's instinct 'would express, in a concrete form, the *relation* of the one to the other' (Bergson 1983: 174).

The difficulty we have in understanding such an incredibly complex relation between the two organisms stems from the assumption that the organism constitutes the fundamental unit of evolution. However, if the relation itself and the material organs which are enfolded within and enact it are regarded as a single component system then the two organisms can be seen as evolving in relation to one another. Bergson considers relations in this respect to be intensive or 'sympathetic'. This sympathetic relation is not only manifest in the actual given situation but orients and governs the evolution of form. In this sense, the organisms act 'through' or within the component system as a whole. For this reason, Bergson agrees with the neo-Lamarckian idea that the actions of the individual organisms have an influence on their evolution. As noted earlier, he also agrees that Weismann's barrier effectively discounts the possibility of simple sensory-motor changes being directly encoded in the DNA. However, he points out that there is no reason why a general form of habit, a specific tendency, cannot be manifest in the genome itself:

The acquired characters we are speaking of are generally habits or
the effects of habit, and at the root of most habits there is a natural
disposition. So that one can always ask whether it is really the habit
acquired by the soma of the individual that is transmitted, or
whether it is not rather a natural aptitude, which existed prior to
the habit. This aptitude would have remained inherent in the germ-
plasm which the individual bears within him, as it was in the
individual himself and consequently in the germ whence he sprang.
(Bergson 1983: 79)

This 'natural disposition' corresponds to a specific tendency orienting
the actions of the organism. Although changes in habit or acquired
characteristics have no direct influence on the actual given genetic
make-up of the organism, they have an effect on the general 'disposition' of the genome, and this broad influence is enfolded in any
variations that arise in reproduction. If the genome is considered to be
'fluid' then this fluidity is not completely amorphous, but has a virtual
orientation, or more accurately, orientations. The genome is expressive
of a multiplicity of 'dispositions'. Such dispositions are in turn not
isolated but 'relational'. From this point of view, not only can the
genes not be isolated from soma but the soma cannot be isolated from
the relations which traverse it.

Furthermore, 'effort' must be accorded, not to some anthropo-
morphic conception of intentionally active organisms but to the
evolutionary process itself:

A hereditary change in a definite direction, which continues to
accumulate and add to itself so as to build up a more and more
complex machine, must certainly be related to some sort of effort,
but to an effort of far greater depth that the individual effort, far
more independent of circumstances . . . (Bergson 1983: 87)

This 'effort' corresponds with what Bergson terms the *élan vital*. It is
within the continuity of duration that life responds to the obstacles
which confront it. As Bergson writes of his own 'vital principle', while
it may not explain very much, at least it reminds us of our ignorance.

The *élan vital* is a sign to affix to our ignorance purely because the nature of duration means that we are always immanent to the evolutionary process. On the other hand, the metaphysics of duration provides the means of transcending the apparent contradictions which divide the likes of neo-Darwinism and neo-Lamarckism, genetics and morphogenesis. Duration is the metaphysical ground of a proper scientific pluralism. Science, however, will never give a complete picture of the whole. The *élan vital* emerges at the limits of science in the aporias, which always leave evolution an open question. The concept of random mutation amounts to a refusal to admit that there is a potential for change in substance which is greater than our understanding. In this sense, the random is nothing but a trope for the fact that the intellect has limits. The only danger in the idea that evolution is a blind automaton of chance and necessity is that it is symptomatic of a refusal to accept that we might have to change the way in which we think in order to apprehend change in its continuity. When evolution is apprehended as an *enduring* process there is no alternative but to accept that evolution is a process which *thinks itself*. The danger Dennett perceives in Darwinism of evolution as a blind force driven by competition is not really all that profound, it is the nihilism of a world without will.

Bergson considers the primary 'disposition' governing the evolution of humanity to be the correlated attributes of the intellect and mechanism. Humanity did not emerge with some transcendent form of reason; rather, the disposition towards utility has oriented human development towards being an 'intelligent' animal. The intellect, Bergson argues, is a machine which has triumphed over mechanism (Bergson 1983: 264). Through the intellect the human has been able to adapt the mechanistic tendencies of nature to its own ends. Mechanism, in this sense, is what defines the human as an animal. Bergson regards the form of mechanism to render the human to be, in one respect, an 'end' of the evolutionary process (Bergson 1983: 265). As the Turing Machine indicates, for example, there is a universal form of mechanism and the intellect is its apotheosis. Seen from this perspective, Dennett's Faustian project is probably the clearest expression of the 'end of man'.

Darwin's Dangerous Idea concludes with a discussion of a Darwinian 'ethics'. In this case, however, Dennett sidesteps the problematic ethical inferences of the 'survival of the fittest', and raises the 'mechanism' of thought to a position equivalent to that of Kantian reason. Neither 'chance and necessity' nor 'natural selection' equate with the 'Law', rather the simple algorithm of 'choice' is raised to the level of a universal ethical imperative. Dennett outlines the future of ethics as follows:

> It is nice to have grizzly bears and wolves living in the wild. They are no longer a menace; we can peacefully coexist, with a little wisdom. The same policy can be discerned in our political tolerance, in religious freedom. You are free to preserve or create any religious creed you wish, so long as it does not become a public menace. We're all on the Earth together, and we have to learn some accommodation . . . (Dennett 1995: 516)

In this passage Dennett reveals the utterly *tendentious* liberalism underlying his entire project. If, as Marx believed, Kant was the 'Adam Smith' of epistemology, making of the transcendental categories a sort of 'hidden hand' of thought, Dennett is the 'Francis Fukuyama' of contemporary philosophy. If liberal capitalism means the end of history for Fukuyama, with Dennett, neo-Darwinism spells the *end of evolution*. The above quotation could be subjected to a good deal of rhetorical analysis but what is most obvious is that Dennett's entire book is aimed at sending 'evolution' to the zoo. The 516 pages preceding this passage, devoted to convincing the reader of the universality of 'chance and necessity', are for the sole purpose of emancipating the liberal subject from 'nature'. This is in line with Bergson's insight that the subject of science constitutes a position which is outside of movement and process. The very subject position of neo-Darwinism is, in this respect, conceived to be outside of evolution: the emancipation from nature is inscribed in its point of view. Bergson regards the numerical subject of science to be the same as that of the liberal subject. Both are abstract and universal. In the sense that neo-Darwinism elides any activity in organisms, liberalism elides any activity in people.

As with 'pure perception', the liberal subject who, in the end, is nothing but a machine for choosing, exists only in theory and not in fact. On the other hand, Dennett's description of the mind as simply a sum of mechanisms or algorithms, a mass of sensory-motor habits, is not simply mistaken, it is the manifestation of a tendency which has become actualized in material relations and continues to do so with increasing rapidity. The subject under capitalism is nothing but a machine for choosing and acting. As mechanism is predicated on the negation of process, the autonomous liberal subject as the bare mechanism of thinking, acting and choosing is predicated on the negation of affectivity. Affectivity is one thing we cannot 'choose'. Where Nietzsche says of the categorical imperative, that it 'smells of cruelty', there is equally an insipid violence in Dennett's 'ethics' of automatism (Nietzsche 1994: 45). In Dennett, the 'knowing' subject is as much devoid of feeling as it is based on class and the 'freedom' of the liberal subject is predicated on economic exclusion.

All species, Bergson argues, in becoming actual 'turn on themselves', behaving as if they were an end rather than an expression of movement. This is equally the case with the human. In this respect, 'man' only succeeds in realizing himself *by abandoning a part of himself along the way*' (Bergson 1983: 266). That which is abandoned is duration itself. The scientific and liberal points of view, the spatialization of time and language's capacity to contain the singular in the given, all express for Bergson the negation of our immanence to the continuity of change. The greatest problem facing the human at present is 'humanism'. The commodification of culture, the mechanization of life, the universal economic subject and the domination of science and technology, are reducing the human to 'quantitative' variations of an abstract category. Dennett's definition of the mind as the 'algorithm of algorithms' exposes precisely where 'difference' is to be found, in the duration of thought and action. Moreover, Dennett's hypermaterialist description of the mind as a mechanism is contained within Bergson's definition of the brain in *Matter and Memory*. The brain corresponds to the mind as seen from the outside and stopped for an instant. As Bergson demonstrates, this perspective leaves out both continuity and affectivity. These two factors correspond to the duration of thought and action, and it is in the duration of the mind that Bergson discerns the potential for transcending the abstract confines of neoliberalism.

CHAPTER 3

Capitalist Tendencies

how the nature of reflective thought
conditions the direction of human evolution

With respect to the current state of things, Marx's analysis of capital appears nothing short of prophetic. Virtually everything he attributes to capital – from its unceasing expansion to globalization, commodity fetishization and automated production, to the increased rapidity of transport and communication – has become a reality. On the other hand, despite the widening gap between rich and poor that Marx also predicted, 'class struggle' appears to be in decline. As Marx foresaw, the wealth and power of those who control the means of production continues to grow disproportionately. However, rather than the 'revolutionary consciousness' that Marx believed would result from this, the political climate we currently see is closer to the opposite.

Generally speaking, it appears that ignorance rather than enlightenment and apathy rather than activism are growing in tandem with the advance of capital. Although capitalism itself and institutions such as the IMF have recently become targets of organized protest, the level of participation is almost negligible in proportion to the predominantly apathetic populace. Instead of being inspired by a clear sense of the ills of capital, protest is predominantly expressed through individual complaints, such as Third World debt and globalization, with very little sense of a viable and collectively desirable alternative. And rather than building and uniting resistance to capital, today's demonstrations, or at least their media representation, have the effect of turning the working classes against themselves.

Even though there are now more 'workers' than ever before, in the absence of any recognizable opposition the term 'working class' loses its meaning. While economically determined class differences undoubtably remain, there is no sense today of any class identifying itself in opposition to the proprietors of capital. It appears, for this reason, that class conflict is not, as Marx thought, the primary motor of capitalism. Which further implies that the wage-relation does not necessarily or directly give rise to alienation. As we are now seeing, deregulation produces more of an urgency to work than a desire for emancipation.

To say the average wage-earner does not suffer alienation is not to deny discontent in today's consumer society. Disaffection, boredom and depression are clearly prevalent in all sectors of contemporary life. What we are not seeing, however, is the enlightenment alienation would bring. Marx expected alienation from material society not only to unite workers as a class but also to serve as the means by which they would come to realize their own creative potential as the source of emancipation. In direct contrast to this, it appears, for the moment at least, that the majority of wage-earners are as willing to work as they are content with commodification.

Although the current social climate questions the validity of concepts such as alienation and class conflict, it does not necessarily undermine either the consistency or relevance of Marx's thought as a whole. In fact, if the role of alienation is diminished then, in his terms, the present state of things is what would be expected. For instance, if the effects of alienation are removed then there will be less constraints on capital the more it expands. As we have seen in recent years, the power of unions and organized labour has decreased at the same time as multinational corporations have become powers unto themselves. In keeping with this, with nothing to counter ideology the material form of society is increasingly accepted as 'natural' rather than a product of human action. If there is anything uniting the wage-earning classes, it lies in their consent that to work is an imperative and the foundation of moral character. As we are currently seeing, it is not the capitalists who are considered parasitic to society, but students, refugees and the unemployed.

If the likes of the United States, Australia and Britain are anything to go by, then the political response to capitalist growth is the inverse of what Marx predicted. For instance, economic development has not strengthened but completely undermined the political division between left and right. The 'free market' is now a political given: the only difference between parties being whether they support capitalism apologetically or not. And while mainstream politics has become increasingly homogenized, political activism has been steadily marginalized and fragmented.

Not only are science and capital becoming increasingly dominant, but they are doing so under their own steam. Following capitalism's much celebrated 'victory' over communism and 'ideology', the free market has been swiftly enveloping the globe. The rapid deregulation witnessed by the West in the last few decades has been paralleled by an equally efficient restructuring of the wider global economy. As things now stand, capital is very close to its goal of a unified world market. At the same time, there have been equally rapid developments in all sectors of science and technology, as well as an increasing expansion of the role of scientific thought in general. Not only has science aided globalization through the development of communication technologies, but through the likes of genetic manipulation it has carried capitalist modes of production into the heart of nature itself.

Even if we wish to refuse ideology, we can see today, that aside from economics itself, the dominant modes of knowledge are all categories of the scientific. To begin with, through technological advancements science has greatly enhanced the development of all modes of capitalist production. In line with this, science has reduced the general perception of the real to bare materiality to such a degree that the nature of material society is now hardly in question. In one way, the present relation we see between thought and capital serves to verify Marx's contention that life determines consciousness. At the same time, there is a lack of any collective sense that consciousness is imposed. Today, more than ever before, destiny is believed to result from individual choice. Directly opposed to what Marx expected therefore, it appears as if the nature of capitalist consciousness is congruent with consciousness in general.

The suspicion that there is something in the nature of consciousness not wholly determined by nurture is further aroused by the remarkably unrevolutionary manner of capital's present phase. Amidst the cultural and social upheavals brought about by globalization and deregulation, the liberal tenets of choice and free will have quietly and smoothly become givens of ordinary life. Even though capital is determining, more than ever before, the entire content of people's lives and accelerating their pace and fragility, it has somehow managed to produce more tacit acceptance than conflict and revolt. One doesn't need to be a Marxist to be surprised at how unshocking the new has turned out to be.

Given that capital's maturation has managed to produce mass conversion to a liberal attitude, we cannot deny Marx's point that the form of objective existence determines that of consciousness. At the same time, the ease of the transition just as equally suggests a congruence between human consciousness and capital. Hence, there must be something within thought that determines the development of capital but is also determined by it.

OBJECTIVITY

Our ability to apprehend the world objectively, or as separate from ourselves, is not simply an accident of thought but, as Bergson has shown, arose as the correlate of our capacity to adapt both ourselves to the world and the world to ourselves. Through the emergence of reflective consciousness, in this sense, the human acquired the ability to see itself acting. And, on the one hand, it is this distance between the self and the self as object that allows us to determine our own actions, thereby releasing human action from the constraints of instinct. On the other hand, the ability to distance ourselves from the world gives us the capacity to fabricate our own environment. On the whole, it is by perceiving things objectively that we are able to adapt the self and the world to one another.

As the source of our adaptability, reflective consciousness can be seen to distance us not only from the world but from the evolutionary process itself. Somewhat paradoxically, it is through our ability to adapt ourselves that we elude the very process through which we came into being. From another perspective, however, in fabricating its own environment, the human can be seen to actualize an aspect of evolution itself. In evolutionary terms, adaptation signifies the process whereby forms and functions are integrated. Through adaptation all modes of change are interrelated, with the enviroment constituting an interconnected whole. The movement of adaptation, therefore, transcends the preservation of difference that results from the struggle to survive. In distancing itself from the world as object, the human has acquired the ability to adapt the world to itself, and in doing so eludes the transcendent movement of evolutionary change.

Properly speaking, human adaptation has two aspects: we adapt the world to ourselves, by manipulating it, and we adapt ourselves to the world, by changing our habits. In the first case, as Bergson has shown, the world that we manipulate is one capable of being divided and rearranged at will. The solid yet divisible content of fabrication is what he refers to as matter. As Bergson insists and the advances and general success of twentieth-century science have only confirmed, there is no need to doubt the existence of the material world. In another sense, however, the continuity of substance precludes the existence of wholly discrete objects. As there is no absolutely vacuous space, nor any complete breaks in time, all modes of substance are united in the continuity of duration.

In the light of this, Bergson has shown that we must conceive matter as potential rather than actual in order to retain both the reality of matter and the continuity of substance. In this sense, matter is less an image of the real and more an ideal towards which substance tends. Quite simply, matter signifies stability, and it is in the nature of material form to endure. However, with respect to the continuity of substance, material form can never be fully actualized. Accordingly, the timeless quality of spatial form is an ideal to which substance tends but never truly reaches.

In line with the above, we can now regard the world we perceive objectively as the actualization of a material order existing potentially in substance. Moreover, the ideal form towards which matter tends is itself actualized as the form of objective consciousness. The reflective self, in this sense, constitutes the framework of perception structuring the space in which we 'see ourselves acting'. Instead of being imposed on reality, therefore, both space and material form are abstracted from reality. As the framework of objective order, reflective consciousness literally serves to frame the real: transforming substance into an aggregate of discrete objects distributed in an abstract space. Consequently, the only thing consciousness adds to the real is negation. However, rather than creating nothingness, in negating the continuity of substance thought actualizes the ideal limits of material form. And since space has been shown to 'admit of degrees', we can now see that the form of reflective consciousness is no longer transcendental but a point of view of substance itself.

The discrete, divisible materiality that makes up the objective world is the basis upon which we fabricate our environment. We adapt the environment to ourselves, in this sense, by rearranging its material components. As the spatial framework of objectivity, reflective consciousness corresponds to the form of material reality. As the correlate of matter, therefore, the reflective self is as flexible as objectivity. Thus, the more we adapt the world, the more it conforms to the structure of our thought.

Obviously, there is more to material order than just form. Processes can also be seen to maintain stability through repetition. Since all sequential processes are contained within the form of mechanism, repetitive order in general can be defined as mechanistic. Mechanism, in this sense, is complementary to material form. As the ideal structure of any step-by-step process, mechanism describes the movement of relations between discrete material elements. Given our ability to predict and control material systems, we can hardly doubt the existence of mechanistic form. Nevertheless, as all mechanistic systems are composed of a sequence of discrete steps, a purely mechanical process can only be an ideal, for continuity precludes any step being completely isolated in space and time. We describe systems as mechanical because they are repeatable, yet no process can be said to repeat itself exactly. Ultimately, the form of mechanism must be seen to be both real and ideal: mechanism exists potentially as the form of repetitive order, and although it is incapable of being actualized in itself, it manifests itself as an ideal towards which substance tends.

Although no process can repeat itself absolutely, systems can be said to seek mechanical repetition in order to maintain stability. Again, as with form, the mechanical order that exists potentially in substance as a tendency is actualized in becoming objective. The order we perceive objectively, for this reason, is by nature ideal while the idea of mechanism is the form of objective thought itself. In essence, mechanical order is objectified by taking the tendency towards mechanism to its ideal limit. As a mechanical process is composed of a series of discrete steps, objectification is achieved through the elision of continuity. Overall, we can say that the elements isolated by the spatial framework of reflective consciousness are in turn united sequentially by the mechanism of objective thought.

All told, the abstract frame of reflective consciousness, together with the mechanism of objective thought, comprise the primary components of the intellect. Rather than imposing order upon the real, the intellect actualizes the ideals of form and mechanism existing potentially in substance. In line with this, the intellect can be compared to what Spinoza termed the 'idea' of the body or extension. In this sense, the ideals of form and mechanism are actualized as the framework and structure of objective thought. While objectification is brought about through negation, rather than adding 'nothing' to the real, the intellect *subtracts* the continuity that exceeds material order.

In actualizing the form of mechanical order, objective thought gives the human the power to free itself from determinism. For this reason, Bergson describes the intellect as 'a machine which somewhat paradoxically triumphs over mechanism' (Bergson 1983: 264). In other words, in conceiving mechanical order, the human distances itself from the order of nature. The more ideas we have of nature, the greater our ability to elude its power. However, more than simply eluding fate, the intellect gives us the capacity to adapt the objective world to the shape of our needs. On the one hand, we fabricate not only material form but also mechanical order – the manipulation of which is the basis of all technological development. On the other hand, the ability to see ourselves act gives us control over our actions, thereby releasing us from the constraints of instinct. As the material complement of thought, the objective self acquires the potential to perform any mechanical task and adapt its motor mechanisms or habits.

In sum, the three fundamental capacities attributable to the intellect, namely the conception of order, the fabrication of matter and a command over action, each contribute to our ability to govern the environment. Although distinct, the three facets are united by the common desire to transcend the immanent forces of evolution and change. Broadly speaking, we distance ourselves from nature by making our environment conform to the structures of objective thought and habit. Rather than proceeding dialectically or in relation to any given forms of thought or human need, our conception, fabrication and adaptation of the world unfold simultaneously. In other words, we adapt ourselves to the world and the world to ourselves at the same time. Despite there being no particular form of human existence, our desire to exert more and more control over the environment, together with the universal conditions for objectivity, give direction to human development in general. Conditioned by the tenets of objectivity, on the one hand, and motivated by our increasing governance of the environment, on the other, the manipulation of the objective world unfolds in the manner of what Bergson terms a 'tendency'.

Somewhat ironically, the word most frequently employed for describing the movement of change is, at the same time, the least defined. The review of any amount of literature will show that the word 'tendency' is the most ubiquitous term in the English language for depicting the direction of movement. And yet, there is tacit consent that a 'tendency' is only a vague approximation, standing in for putatively more precise and 'scientific' models. However, it is becoming increasingly evident that classical physics is not only too precise, today's 'chaotic' and 'fuzzy' alternatives can themselves only ever approximate the movement of change. Rather than giving direction to change, chaos theories in general only manage to add chance to necessity, removing all momentum from movement itself. In contrast, as Bergson insists, the idea of the tendency offers a precise intuitive sense of how change can have direction without being wholly determined. Moreover, in conceiving movement as directed from within we are able to escape the confines of order and disorder. In tending to be, the movement of change remains continuous rather than recursive or dialectical.

It is in this sense that Bergson perceives a broad tendency directing human development towards the increased fabrication of the material environment. The potential to control the environment, on the one hand, and the general form of objectivity, on the other, have given rise to a tendency within human action itself. To varying degrees, every human habitat is becoming increasingly material and at the same time structured in conformity with the conditions of objective thought. Quite simply, we tend as a species to fabricate our own environment and mechanize our actions, and although there is no universal form of human existence, the form of objective reality is itself universal by nature.

REPRESENTATION

In actuality, the continuity 'wherein we act' is as indivisible as life itself. Neither thought nor action, therefore, can be wholly mechanized since they cannot be reduced to series of isolated steps. Incapable of removing ourselves completely from continuity, we are similarly precluded from distancing ourselves from change.

While thought is continuous in reality, language gives it the appearance of being composed of wholly discrete elements. In this case, however, it is not so much thought that divides language as language that divides thought. Because language acts as both the subject and object of thought, we are led to assume that thought and language are the same: that each consists entirely of words and the relations between them. Moreover, it is language which, as a form of representation, allows us to perceive the world as if it is entirely objective. By naming objects, actions and qualities, we isolate them, both from one another and from change. And by dividing the world into discrete parts, we are then able to reorder it in thought, for instance, and rearrange it at will.

Ultimately, when we represent the world we effectively take objectivity to its ideal limit. In fact, as Bergson has shown, the abstract frame through which we perceive the world objectively turns out to be the form of representation itself. Representing an objective phenomenon is equivalent to actualizing its form or, in other words, capturing the object in a frame and thus, detaching it from its surroundings. A camera, for instance, takes perception to its ideal limit: whenever we 'take a picture' we literally actualize the framework of reflective consciousness by 'freezing' a frame in time. In a similar vein, language takes the frame of reflective thought to its abstract limit by actualizing it in the idea of the class or empty set. When we name a quality, action or object, we refer to it as the manifestation of an abstract form, which is, in turn, equivalent to the class through which we isolate actual modes of the thing. The name tree, for example, denotes an ideal, equivalent not only to the set of all trees but to the class of all classes of tree.

Although obviously deriving from thought, it is in fact representation that determines the way we think. To begin with, the form of representation is itself the actualization of the abstract frame of reflective thought. The frame is the means by which we isolate things in space and time. As the frame of reflective thought in itself, the form of representation is entirely spatial. Through representation, therefore, all differences are rendered spatially distinct and difference itself becomes spatialized.

Not only are things, qualities and processes represented as spatially distinct, their differing forms or classes are isolated from one another in the ideal or logical space of thought. Moreover, the form of the class concept is itself of a timeless or entirely spatial nature. The class corresponding to any name, for instance, is conceived as existing outside of time. The name, furthermore, refers to an object which is wholly actual and removed from the continuity of change. Other than qualitative, representation presents all differences as spatial variations in quantity. The idea of quantity can be further reduced to spatial magnitude, with classes differing either in scales of spatial containment, or by the number of elements they contain.

With language we can represent all quantitative and qualitative differences in terms of sets and classes. Number, for example, has been shown to derive from the idea of a set. If we equate all empty sets with zero or the class of nothing, we can then construct any numerical sequence by generating series of sets of sets where one is the class of zero, two is the class of one, and so forth. From this perspective, number is essentially no different than name, inasmuch as both 'two' and 'tree' represent the class of all classes of a qualitatively distinct thing. It is this common ground to numerical and descriptive languages that allows them to be used in combination to represent differences within and between qualities. With something like '25 bananas' we simply enumerate the class of thing, while with a 'big car', we bring quantitative distinction to the class itself. Through number we can also represent differences between distinct qualities: as is clearly illustrated by the periodic table, where number not only allows us to order elements sequentially but distinguish classes within the table as a whole.

Owing to the fact that we think in language, the form of representation must be seen to condition the intellect as a whole. By actualizing the framework of reflective consciousness, for instance, representation is that which makes the intellect the mechanism of thought. Representation, in this sense, not only allows us to conceive forms and qualities as if they are wholly actual but also actions and processes as if they are perfectly repeatable. As Bergson consistently demonstrates, the intellect does not, as Kant believed, impose order on the world. The likes of the periodic table and DNA should be proof enough that order has an independent existence. Order itself, however, does not exist in the actual form in which we perceive it, but as a potential or tendency that the intellect, or more accurately representation, brings to its ideal limit. The idealism of thought, as Bergson describes it, is its hyperbolic precision.

The wholly actualized objective order presupposed by representation is what Bergson refers to as matter. All in all, matter signifies the tendency within substance towards stability and order. In terms of representation, matter is synonymous with objectivity and constitutes the world in which we 'see ourselves acting'. As our ability to perceive objectively is tied to our command of self and world, the greater our representation of reality, the greater our control. Most significantly, however, our greatest potential for controlling the environment comes from our ability to adapt material reality and our thought to one another. By mechanizing the environment through our actions and technology, material reality becomes increasingly structured in conformity with our thought. Overall, the form of representation actualizes our tendency to control the world. As Bergson has argued, the human environment is becoming increasingly material and human thought more intellectual.

The rapid advances made in science during the late nineteenth century were, for Bergson, the clearest indication of the tendency towards increased materialization. In line with this, he considered science to be the primary motor of change and further predicted that its growth would accelerate. In terms of science, at least, history has confirmed, and continues to confirm, his analysis. From quantum physics to genetics to the big bang, science is approaching a complete representation of objective reality. While many still believe in a science disinterestedly seeking to improve our understanding of the universe, there are few scientific developments that can, in actuality, be separated from our desire to predict, control and manipulate the material world. From meteorology to medicine, science aims to keep us one step ahead of nature; advances in genetic science now give us the ability to engineer life itself, while through technological development in general we shape the material environment to the structure of our habits. Moreover, in keeping with Bergson's observations, science continues to reduce the real almost entirely to matter. Not only life but human consciousness and even personality, are now regarded as governed solely by the mechanics of the DNA. With the likes of plastic surgery, genetic engineering and pharmaceuticals, science has reduced life to an almost bare materiality – one that can be manipulated at will.

The only shortcoming in Bergson's analysis is that today science is not alone in making our lives increasingly material. In fact, many of the above changes could just as easily be attributed to capitalism. One could say that the tendency towards materiality is a direct result of capital itself. However, what else is capitalism but the process whereby life is increasingly objectified, and human actions progressively mechanized and integrated into an unified economic order? In this sense, capitalism seems to be unfolding in precisely the same manner Bergson describes the material tendency governing human development. While science and capital are complicit in many areas, the two have clearly independent aims.

Although advances in science and technology are obviously implicated in today's economic changes, science does not, as Marx believed, stem from and serve the interests of capital alone. Quite simply, scientific enquiry is not in itself predicated on economic returns. In order to increase our knowledge beyond the known, science must be free from the demands of profitability. Ironically, however, it is the autonomy of science that is of the greatest value to capital. By increasing our knowledge of the structure and composition of natural forms and processes, for instance, science aids the expansion of capitalist modes of production. Following the discovery of the DNA, we now have the ability to increase genetically the 'efficiency' of almost any agricultural product. Similarly, arising from the efforts of scientists to better communicate, the Internet has become one of the major events in the history of capital. It seems today that wherever science goes capital follows.

While science and capitalism share numerous economic and technological affinities, their ultimate foundation lies in the form of representation. The very existence of modern science is inseparable from the modes of representation it employs: combining language and number, for instance, science represents, analyses and reconstructs the world as a sum of units. As we have seen, the form of representation conditions science as a whole, transforming the real into a purely material actuality where all qualities are spatially distinct and all quantities spatially determined. The same can be said of the ultimate 'unit' of capital: the commodity. The commodity form is no different to any other mode of representation, for as with number, language and the scientific unit, it allows us to isolate distinct qualities while at the same time integrating their differences into a unified objective order. Through the process of commodification, capital continually reconstructs the world in the form of its representation. While as commodities, objects and actions are isolated from one another, they are, at the same time, integrated within the unified space of quantity.

Overall, science and capital must be seen as developing in tandem. On the one hand, by broadening our representation of the objective world and rearranging its order to suit our needs, advances in science appear to give us increased control over our destinies. The expansion of capital, on the other hand, is transforming the human environment into a progressively unified system. Together, the developments of science and capital express an even broader tendency: one which has as its end a world completely adapted to the human and an humanity completely adapted to its world. Ultimately, we are heading towards an humanity and an environment whose 'nature' is indistinguishable from its representation.

COMMODIFICATION AND US

More than simply the making of money, capitalism constitutes a system which progressively integrates the production, distribution and consumption of the objects of human need into an unified economic order. As a whole, capitalism is the overall process through which the environment and human existence are entirely adapted to one another. From this perspective, capital evolves as a wholly integrated order. As a totality, the growth of capital is not something we directly control. While there are obvious imbalances of power, the life of a capitalist is, in the end, no less a part of capital than someone who is unemployed. Similarly, capitalism cannot be reduced to a particular economic system: the nature of capital simply expresses the logic of money itself.

The fundamental unit of capital is the commodity: the simplest form being money which can be bought and sold like any other goods. As a measure of value as well as a means of exchange, money is the basis of the commodity form. In terms of exchange, money serves as a universal equivalent, allowing any object or quality to be exchanged for any other. As a consequence, there are no relations of exchange in capitalism not mediated by money. Hence, the monetary relation has the effect of atomizing difference. However, since all qualities are translated into variations in quantity, money is the basis upon which capital becomes an unified entity, allowing anything to be integrated into a singular economic space and time.

As a measure of value, money represents the quantity for which qualitative differences can be exchanged. Ignoring for the moment the origin of value, the monetary figure attributed to a commodity does not refer directly to the thing; otherwise everything would have its own price, but to the object as a representation of its class. Value, therefore, is not simply added to an independent object: the commodity form fuses the qualitative class of an object with the form of quantitative difference — as terms such as 'two-dollar pen' and 'ten-dollar pizza' illustrate.

The overall means to capital's expansion is profit, which is both the aim and the source of investment. Essentially, profit is the difference between the price for which a commodity is sold and the overall cost of its production. For profitability to improve, therefore, there must be either an increase in the volume of sales or a decrease in the cost of production. Furthermore, the potential for profit increases as the total volume of commodities expands. As a result, the marketplace is always growing and the range of commodities forever increasing. The goal of capital is, in the end, to commodify not only the total number of lives but the totality of life. Through the reinvestment of profit into production, all modes of production are drawn into the capitalist process. Predicated on quantitative factors, capitalist production is essentially mechanistic and as an effect of the demand for ever lower costs, the ideal form of production becomes the form of mechanism itself.

As capital grows, the composition of existence becomes increasingly commodified. Not only our personal effects but the entire production process, services and work, are pieced together with individual commodities. A commodity is something that fits in with capitalism as a whole expressing not only the needs of human existence but the needs of capital itself. From this perspective we can discern the nature of capital from within the nature of the commodity form. Bringing together qualitative and quantitative difference, the commodity combines the characteristics of language and number. As in language, commodification renders all qualitative differences spatially distinct, while as in number, difference itself is spatialized. These fundamental attributes of the commodity form can be seen to condition the whole of capitalist existence. Moreover, from this point of view we can see how representation is intrinsic to science and capital.

The motor of capital's expansion and commodity development is competition. Through the competition to capture demand, commodities become separated from one another as classes. At the same time, however, as producers vie to supply the same need, competing commodities are unified as a class. Competition, in this sense, creates an ideal common to each member of the class while being at the same time beyond them. As commodities are isolated from one another by the monetary relation, each commodity is materially representative of itself as a class. Accordingly, the ideal form presupposed in the representation of an object becomes increasingly reified in the commodity's material form.

As form cannot be represented in any other way than by the

material form of the thing itself, each commodity is both an example of its own form and a model of what it should be. Today's banana has been crossbred, genetically altered and chemically ripened so as to look and taste 'more like' a banana. Over time, within any class of commodity the number of competitors decreases, as only those selling the largest number survive. From this perspective, competition and development lead to needs and their objects becoming moulded to one another: both the form of demand and the commodity class become increasingly standardized. The only difference between mobile phones is their colour and shape. The most notable illustration is agriculture, where practically every product today, from the avocado to the courgette, has been transformed from a class of multiple and varying types into an almost uniform variety.

Within any one class of commodity, what has traditionally been referred to as 'quality' becomes increasingly determined in terms of quantity. The commodity at the bottom end of any class corresponds to the essential idea of the thing, capable of fulfilling its basic function as well as being the cheapest to produce. A 'no frills' airline will get you from A to B, but it is you who supply the food and entertainment. MacDonalds supplies the basic idea of food combining bread, meat and potatoes with the essential elements of taste, salty and sweet. Progressing up the scale of value within any class one will inevitably find that the basic form is complemented by additional uses and effects and a higher cost of production.

Predicated on creating ever more efficient manufacturing processes, the capitalist mode of production presupposes mechanization and the creation of a standardized model. In order to be produced uniformly the commodity must conform to an objective idea divisible into parts capable of being independently manufactured. Furthermore, through mechanization production can be reduced to a set of individual stages capable of being broken down into a series of steps and integrated into a unified process. The capitalist production process, in this sense, corresponds directly with the form of objective action or habit. For this reason, not only is the manufacturing process increasingly mechanized, all forms of labour, from the point of view of capital, are specialized and composed of nothing more than a mechanical series of steps.

The clearest illustration of the capitalist mode of production appears in the instances where labour is the commodity. Conditioned entirely by representation, the objective activity is determined in relation to a model or abstract idea: in the sense that an Italian waiter is expected to act *like* an Italian waiter. Similarly, with the American 'Charter school' system, which is based on the idea of schooling as a profit-making business, the packaging of education for sale like any other commodity has resulted in the mechanization of learning. Not only is the school designed to conform to a model of the 'ideal' education, the curriculum is completely standardized and each lesson entirely prewritten. In class the 'teacher' simply recites the day's programme, allowing the hire of unqualified staff and creating the potential to lower the cost of production.

All commodities are ultimately integrated into an unified and self-sustaining social order. With regard to capital, education for instance, serves to create an able workforce capable of fulfilling the projected needs of capitalist production. Ultimately, every commodity fulfils a corresponding need which in turn expresses the requirement of capital as a functioning social whole. Television fills the time between work and sleep, while the leisure industry provides rest and recuperation for the general workforce, and so on and so on.

On the other hand, in its progression capitalism draws from scientific research, selecting those findings that either aid the production process or meet the technological needs of the time. Through the independent discovery of the DNA and the subsequent advances in genetic science, the capitalist production process has now expanded into life itself. No different from any other commodity, crops are genetically altered to increase their efficiency and output. Alternatively, although the Internet appears to have been created unintentionally, it proved almost immediately to be the perfect aid to capitalism's already global tendencies. Following the arrival of the Internet, we have seen a new era emerge in distribution where shopping no longer requires shops and through the commodification of information, business has the potential to become truly global.

While capitalism is often said to champion the virtues of novelty and change, the movement of change within capital itself is clearly not directionless. Commodity development is neither the result of blind invention nor dependent simply on the vagaries of choice and consumer demand. All changes within the market and the means of production are implicated within the overall movement of capital's expansion. As a consequence, change is manifest in the form of new commodities. Rather than just an object of consumption, the commodity constitutes a component, the total sum of which makes up a self-sustaining machine. In addition to the Internet, the mobile phone, digital camera, low-cost scanner, CD ROM, fibre-optics, and so on and so on, all make up the era of global communications and information. Not only has this paved the way for globalization, it has provided the perfect means for uniting an increasingly atomized population. Moreover, as all forms of electronic communication are mediated by the monetary relation, we find both language and its use are increasingly determined by representation. As a medium, language is tending towards uniformity, where English is regarded as the language of commerce and regional languages and dialects fall outside the competition. What is more, meaning is now synonymous with information and, as computer translation programs presuppose, reducible to the words alone.

Due to the nature of representation, inherent in the commodity, any object can be exchanged for any other and all forms of mechanical processes linked together. It is ultimately commodification, in this sense, that allows capitalism to function as a coordinated whole. In addition to creating an unified material economy, commodification provides the basis upon which capitalism maintains social unity. Labour is the one commodity possessed by the subject. Quite simply, by exchanging their time for money, the worker is both integrated into the production process and given the means to consume. As a consequence, the wage is the fluid of capitalist society. More than simply sustaining the workforce, the wage is the basis to consumption and thus, logically, to production. Aside from owning capital, the wage is the only means of sustaining existence within capitalism. The commodification of labour is the means through which capitalism functions as a social whole. To illustrate the fact that work relates not simply to production but to capitalism itself as a social entity, one only need note that even though a large proportion of manual labour has been replaced by technological mechanization, there is not less but more work today than ever before.

Full employment is not necessarily the means to achieving the highest level of production. In fact, productivity is more likely to improve the smaller the workforce and the greater the automation. Nevertheless, we find work being continually created and full employment a goal forever in sight. The dismantling of the welfare state has revealed the creation of work to be capitalism's only method for gaining social control. Although schemes such as 'work for the dole', suggest that work is imposed so as to maintain order, the foundation of social unity under capital derives far more efficiently from what is an essentially tacit imperative. Within capitalism, work is elevated to a moral obligation where the individual is responsible for the functioning of the whole.

Being a commodity, the nature of work or, in other words, 'labour' is conditioned by the form of representation. Just as the value of an object refers not to the thing but its class, so too the value of labour presupposes a general form, what Marx, for instance, terms 'abstract labour'. On the one hand, labour is valued purely in relation to the quantity of time it takes. On the other hand, since any labour practice is essentially a series of steps, abstract labour is reducible to the 'mechanism of mechanisms'. Accordingly, labour in general is equivalent to the point of view from which 'we see ourselves act'. In this sense, abstract labour is the subject of capital itself.

Through commodification it is not only the value of labour time that is quantified but the actual time in which labour is practised. In the workplace, the time required by the task supersedes and elides the duration in which one lives. Determined wholly by the objective production process, labour is then an entirely objective action, which is not only conducted from an abstract point of view, in terms of capital, but demands that one act outside oneself. What is more, being the objective point of view itself, the 'mechanism of mechanisms' is not only the subject of labour but the subject of capitalism in general. As the objective economy of capital is composed exclusively of discrete elements and mechanical processes, the abstract 'mechanistic' subject links together the pieces and movements of life. Life in capitalism is an essentially objective existence, where getting out of bed, eating breakfast, catching the bus, going to work, watching television, returning to bed, Friday night, office parties and holidays are determined by the whole as much as being determined by us. Capitalism, therefore, demands we submit our lives to the demands of the objective order – on the understanding that in acting for it, we are acting for ourselves. This assumption is the basis of capitalism's fundamental moral imperative: the obligation to work. Although it is the basis upon which the concepts of responsibility and duty lie, the imperative itself is irrational, in the end its only ground being to state, as Bergson writes, that 'you must because you must'.

The more capitalism advances, the imperative to work and the mechanistic nature of life appear less imposed and more and more in keeping with the way we act in the world. Because the commodity form derives from representation, commodification has the effect of bringing the structure of objectivity in line with that of reflective thought. When we represent the world we are not imposing order, we are taking objectivity to its ideal limit. The form of representation, in this sense, signifies the abstract ideal of reflective thought. As the framework of perception, the reflective self comprises the space in which material forms and qualities are distinguished and distributed. Similarly, reflective thought is in itself the space within which we conceive abstract form and order. Consequently, the more commodified life becomes, the more material existence corresponds to the structure of objective thought. Capitalism is made up of discrete material entities and mechanistic processes distributed within an abstract and quantified space and time. That there is little difference between cultures in capitalism is growing. When you move to New York, having grown up in Munich, you still know how to make a phone call, use a bus, train or taxi and order food; we now expect things to be more the same.

In sum, conditioned by the form of representation, capitalism, in tandem with science, is continually adapting the material world and the objective human subject to one another. As is now undeniable in its evidence, the world as a whole is being governed by a tendency that is transforming the environment into an unified material order in complete concert with the form of human thought, action and necessity. Humanity, in this sense, is not so much bringing the world under its control but is transforming both the world and itself into a mechanism for existing. Illustrated by the likes of ecotourism and the notion of the 'carbon sink', where the cliché of nature has become a commodity, there is no nature existent today that does not reflect the form of human representation. In the end, 'nature' itself will be nothing more than a machine whose sole function is to perpetuate the material image of humanity. The surest testament that this may be inevitable is the fact that even to suggest such a thing will be deemed absurd, conspiratorial, fanciful, left-wing, substanceless, pessimistic, paranoid or naïve in assuming it could ever be otherwise.

A NATURAL IDEOLOGY

The fact that Marx's concept of alienation may be flawed gives no cause for celebration. As we are now seeing, in the absence of alienation the expansion of capital accelerates in proportion with the decline in political awareness. In keeping with its image as the 'end of ideology', capitalist society is now generally assumed to be 'natural'. With liberal subjectivity transcending class differences, political opposition has become marginalized and dismissed as irresponsible romanticism.

Ironically, the 'naturalness' of material society is precisely what Marx defined as ideology, for what appears to be the natural order of capital is, in actuality, determined by the logic of the commodity form. As consciousness is, according to Marx, wholly conditioned by material order, it is in the interests of the ruling class to encourage belief in those ideas, such as free will and materialism, that support capital's natural image. Conversely, Marx believed that alienation from material society would create an awareness of the 'false consciousness' of capitalist subjectivity.

Despite the failed appearance of a revolutionary consciousness, Marxist thought has yet to acknowledge any relation between the structure of capital and the nature of consciousness. Michael Hardt and Antonio Negri, for instance, contend that the, in their terms, 'bizarre' naturalness of capitalism, 'is a pure and simple mystification' which we must 'disabuse ourselves of . . . right away' (Hardt and Negri 1994:

386–7). Unfortunately, however, until we recognize the role consciousness plays in determining material order, the nature of capitalism will continue to mystify us.

Driven by the dual forces of capitalism and science, the materiality of existence and reflective thought must be seen to unfold *in tandem*, directed by the conditions of objectivity and the nature of its representation. The more objective life is regulated by quantitative measures, governed by mechanical processes and directed towards distinct objects in space, the more it corresponds with the abstract ideal of reflective consciousness. As a consequence, not only does the world in which 'we see ourselves acting' conform more with our actions and habits, but material order and the scientific image of nature are increasingly moulded to one another.

Being of the same nature, science functions as the unwitting but effective support of capitalist existence. In practically every introduction to chaos theory, for instance, the stock market is described as an example of self-determining and, therefore, natural order. Just as chance has become the motor of creation, the lottery has replaced redemption as a source of hope. (The idealism of Christian theology, on the other hand, allows it to coexist alongside material existence, providing capital with an endless pool of voluntary labour.) Darwinism, however, remains the clearest support of both the mechanics and ethics of capital – the process of natural selection is now thought to demonstrate the inevitability of competition and market forces. The business world, in this sense, constitutes an ongoing struggle where only the fittest survive. In tune with the strong Darwinian line, not only are alternatives to capital wishful thinking, any form of economic intervention can only upset the 'natural' course of things.

The ideological nature of the contemporary episteme is first intimated in the contradictory images of liberty and determinism currently associated with capitalism and science. On the one hand, freedom of choice is proclaimed as the moral foundation of the free market while, on the other, the biomedical sciences tell us destiny is genetically determined. Besides hereditary diseases and physical traits, there is a growing tendency within fields such as sociobiology and clinical, criminal and neuropsychology, to assign genetic origins to behaviour. According to current research, any predilection, be it criminality, addiction, intelligence or contentment, can be attributed to the make-up of an individual's DNA. In the end, free will and determinism are equally tautological: smokers are said to choose smoking because they smoke, while addicts are said to have 'addictive' genes because they are addicts. Despite the contradictions, liberal freedom and genetic determinism are now called upon wherever they suit.

In addition to the Darwinian idea that it is the 'fittest' who succeed and the 'weak' who fail, we hear today that addicts are supposedly predisposed to addiction in the same way that entrepreneurs are destined to have a 'natural' flair for business, intellectuals are born intelligent and murderers have a gene for violence, etc. Science, in this respect, serves to legitimate the 'nature' of actuality. Delimiting behavioural and social traits solely to the individual's genetic 'facticity' has the effect of eliding any relation between behaviour and the environment, thereby providing a concrete foundation to the atomized, abstract subject of capital. Moreover, the Human Genome Project has played a major part in establishing the idea that difference is wholly material. The project's much celebrated completion further implies that the composition of humanity itself is in some way 'complete'. In contrast to the fact that the genetic make-up of each individual is different, the supposed 'mapping' of the entire human genome is predicated on an idealized and universal model. This genetic 'every-man', provides the perfect bodily counterpart for the equally universal, though ideal, liberal mind.

In keeping with the form of abstract labour, the mechanical functioning of both body and mind constitute the ideal goals of health. Anything that impedes the capacity to work and perform mechanistic tasks, and anything that upsets the ability to adapt to the demands of objective life are considered pathologies. The ideal body is now equivalent to a mechanical Barbie, where the healthy subject is expected to play golf into her nineties and for whom ageing is a form of disease. The more employers and life insurers favour the fit, the more it becomes apparent that eugenics is inherent to the very form of capitalism and science.

Not only must the body maintain a normal standard of health but the workings of the brain must not interfere with daily routine. Denied any value as a statement on life, the affections have become completely pathologized. It is here that contemporary medicine has been of enormous support to capital's imperative of 'self-control'. The massive commodification and proliferation of antidepressants and tranquillizers, for example, even though of great help to many, are predicated on the individuation and materialization of affectivity. With emotional and affective states in general being treated as if they result solely from the individual's chemistry, medicine is seen to provide the means for correcting faults of nature, not the subject's state of affairs. Modern psychiatry and pharmacology reveal the ellision of affectivity to be today's prevailing mode of sensibility.

The complicity between material order and the structure of thought is further reflected in the sudden and virtually ubiquitous acceptance of liberal subjectivity. In a matter of decades, the idea of choice has shifted from being the conceptual basis of liberalist politics to being an almost universal assumption. Every act and its corresponding object, be it smoking or sexuality, is now tacitly assumed to be a matter of choice. The presumption has become so pervasive, we find the likes of happiness, suicide and fame even being referred to as 'choices'. Despite the many shortcomings apparent in its contemporary usage, the acceptance of agency reflects the increasing 'objectification' of existence. As life becomes more material and objectively determined, the more it is conducted from an increasingly abstract, reflective point of view. Being the means through which the subject distinguishes itself from both self and world, reflective consciousness creates the impression that the mind is spatially distinct from the body. The more life is enacted from the reflective point of view, the more it appears *as if* the mind is able to act *on* the body and that the self has control over the will. As objectivity is made up of discrete material forms and processes, the self appears to have control over the will and determine which choices to make and what steps to take in life.

In actuality, choice is more the basis of political responsibility than freedom. Just as many defend their choice to smoke as do those who wish to make smokers responsible for their health care. Although the 'freedom' of choice conflicts with scientific determinism, it has the same effect of individuating responsibility. The same idea of choice that some use in defence of their right to smoke and take drugs is employed by health insurers to defend their right to impose extra charges on smokers and politicians who wish to have drug-users denied free health care. As there are now as many who defend their choices as those who condemn the choosers, it is clear that choice is not so much a faculty as it is the basis to conceptions of right and responsibility. Just as premeditation is assumed in law, to say someone chooses to be unemployed is simply the basis upon which to judge them.

Rather than the basis of 'freedom', liberalism represents the central normative force of capital. Choice is not so much an option as it is an imperative that simply decrees that 'you must because you must' (Bergson 1977: 25). Through the individuation of 'self-control', choice enables the 'self-organization' of the entire economic machine. Instead of the government, it is the subject who orders itself to get a job, get married, have children, go shopping, buy a house, etc. Ironically, the more capital determines life, the less control one has over life and action. As we are clearly witnessing, the more freedom is assumed, the more one is obliged to conform to the objective order of material society and choose what the economy has to offer. Accordingly, as Bergson writes: 'Hence our life unfolds in space rather than in time; we live for the external world rather than for ourselves; we speak rather than think; we 'are acted' rather than act ourselves' (Bergson 1919: 231). When existence is determined economically and life is governed by work, one is obliged to live 'outside oneself', and conform to the mechanistic and chronological routines of the objective world.

Since capitalist society is composed entirely of commodities and order is maintained through the economic integration of production and consumption, choosing commodities, or shopping, becomes just as much an imperative as work. Consumption is, of course, the motor of the economy and in order to maintain a constantly increasing level of production it is not only essential for the economy to expand but for consumers to purchase any 'new' commodities that come onto the market. The ongoing demand for 'difference' has lead to the material basis of virtually every culture and the entire history of art becoming reduced to commodities. While this provides a source of entertainment for the West, the material dissolution of cultures also enables capitalist production to expand throughout the globe. In one sense, economic liberalism is a social and political 'imperative', but, in another, the ease with which liberalism has spread throughout the globe signals the complicity between the form of reflective consciousness and the impression of agency.

Although commodity fetishism appears to be driven by the desire for change for its own sake, the transformation of the material form of commodities is not without direction. All new types of commodity must fit into the overall structure of the economy as well as fulfil the requirements of capital's continued growth. Scientific development, in this respect, has been constantly integrated into material existence. The influence of expansion itself, together with the demand for increasingly efficient production and distribution, has created a demand for increasingly rapid communications and transport. The development of forms of rapid transport and mass distribution has steadily 'reduced' the size of the globe. Similarly, communications technologies have brought people together at the same time as supporting the tendency towards individuation. The more technology becomes integral to material existence, the more it becomes imperative to keep up with change, as each generation leaves the earlier one behind. With virtually every 'working' person in the Western world now integrated into the communications network, it is now possible to live the greater part of one's life without making physical contact.

As life becomes ever more economically determined, the reflective self becomes increasingly separated from sensibility since the demands of the objective order by nature conflict with any 'subjective' desires. In a similar fashion, sensibility, affectivity and desire are all absent from the liberal conception of the subject, whose freedom is due to being detached from the 'will'. As economic existence demands that one act outside oneself, the elision, repression and regulation of sensibility represents both an effect and a condition of the current social order. The only way to sustain existence in capitalist society is to submit to the imperative to work and correlate one's 'habit in general' to the demands of the economy. Moreover, the fact that life is objectively determined creates something of an affective vacuum. The only way to fill in time is either to work or be entertained. Accordingly, in keeping with the imperative to work, success is now the equivalent of being 'cash-rich and time-poor'. Outside of work, capital's primary aim is to fill in time. In this respect, life is quickly imitating art, in daily life, as in the cinema, watching television or playing a computer game, one's attention is constantly directed towards the future, 'suspended' in expectation of what will happen next.

As the objective order comes to determine the whole of existence, the social becomes an increasingly unified and self-governing economic order. However, although order is maintained through the individuation of 'self-control' and time is filled with work and play, the fact that life is conducted from the abstract position of the worker and consumer in general leaves the subject and the social vulnerable to the voice of desire. The bare mechanical repetition of difference and the monotony of work and time leaves room for boredom, stress and general disaffection. Furthermore, as unity is founded on the purely abstract form of the exchange relation, the social is left without a collective identity. It is here that the imperative to shop and work becomes enforced through the individuation of fear. The more capital determines the social, the more submission to the objective order becomes a necessity. As work is the sole source of income, losing one's job carries the threat of social exclusion. The general fear of unemployment is promoted through images of homelessness, while the imperative to work hard and stay employed is encouraged by the constant threat of economic downturn. In all, financial blacklisting and economic exclusion remain forever in the shadow of employment and solvency.

Along with the very real threat of economic ruin, the media has created a virtual wall of fear around every citizen as well as every free market society. At the same time as being entertained, the working are now fed images of criminality and terror. The individual, in this respect, despite his isolation, is encouraged to be wary of strangers and keep his property secure. With the threat now extending to the existence of evildoers intent on destroying free society, working hard, paying tax and shopping become the equivalent of political acts. Simply by staying alive, the liberal individual is able to take pride in his contribution to maintaining the 'freedom' of the social whole.

As capital becomes more unified, the fact that the economy alone defines order means that the social becomes progressively divided from its other. Anything that cannot become integrated into the social order ends up being excluded and negatively defined as underdeveloped, primitive, unemployed and criminal, etc. Despite the fact unemployment is a part of capitalism itself, those without work are labelled lazy and, as with 'dole cheats', often used as scapegoats in times of economic change. In addition to economic order, social and political order are maintained through the law. Today, anything that upsets the economic order of things, no matter what its cause, is deemed to be irresponsible if not criminal. On the grounds that everyone within capitalist society has the same opportunities to find work and generally choose a life, there is now increasingly less sympathy with anything that transgresses either economic, civil or criminal law. The more capital extends into and transforms other societies, and the more rigid the demands of economic existence become, we find that the law becomes increasingly brutal. 'Zero tolerance' is now used to clear the homeless away from middle-class areas; those who are unable to bend to the demands of the economy are now jailed sometimes for quite minor offences. On the national level, hysteria now surrounds the threat of asylum-seekers and refugees who, labelled parasites and criminals, are imprisoned without charge and even pushed back out to sea on sinking boats. State communist societies are excluded from the global economy and military pressure placed where religion interferes with economic liberalism. In all, the world is being transformed into a single economic machine, constantly at war with anything it is unable to integrate within itself.

Not only the 'logic' of capital but all forms of representation derive from and reflect the structure of reflective thought. For this reason, as capital advances the entire social machine comes to complement and support the maintenance of economic unity. With capital assuring a majority of the population a comfortable income, 'democratic' government is steadily reduced to managing capital. At the same time, because public opinion also becomes the sole measure of value, all means of combating the threats to order, from carpet-bombing fifteen-year-old youths to giving life-sentences to petty thieves, are carried out under the sanction of the 'moral majority'. As it is in the very nature of the current social order to expand, we now find that any degree of direct opposition to capital, science or their globalizing effects, comes under attack and eventually makes the whole even stronger.

CHAPTER 4

Metaphysics beyond Marx

the substance of aesthetics, culture and sensibility

Although Marx was certainly correct in his account of the continued expansion of capitalism, politically, things appear to be the reverse of what he predicted. Instead of a class conflict, liberal subjectivity now transcends any division between capitalist and worker. Rather than revolutionary consciousness, there is a growing hostility amongst today's broad 'middle class' towards politics altogether.

Now that 'civilization' is a synonym of capitalist democracy, anything critical of the current state of things is branded 'radical' and dismissed as irresponsible romanticism. Since democracy has become the 'political wing' of capitalism, the media, the state and the 'general public' have become violently intolerant of anything but 'personal opinion'. Because capitalism is the social order, 'anti-capitalism' has become a convenient and cogent means of containing any political critique of capital, or science or democracy, whatever. Intimidated by the threat of 'disorder', the working class now accepts anti-capitalism as legitimation for any amount of police or military violence.

Since within capitalist society everything appears to be a matter of choice and everyone is supposedly equal in the eyes of the law and have the same economic opportunities, it has become generally accepted that criminals and illegal immigrants are simply greedy and the unemployed, lazy. Furthermore, because people appear to make their own conscious 'life-choices', few question the fact that the most powerful capitalist country houses a quarter of the world's prison inmates, a large percentage of whom are a formally enslaved minority. As the liberalist ideal of the universal 'right' to 'free' choice is the only political position that capitalism and democracy allow, whether white, black, gay or Muslim, one has no alternative but to follow the 'straight and narrow', get a job, get married, buy a house, get connected and watch television. As the only real political choice of any minority is to 'get a job', virtually every political movement of the past has dissolved into individual 'responsibility'.

The fact that capitalism is now in actuality synonymous with social order, means that the exclusion and entrapment of any alternative to capital as 'other' is part of the very logic of representation. Not only does the prefix 'anti' set politics itself against capitalism, globalization or science, it conveniently allows all positions to be bracketed together, along with alternative, romantic and disordered. As the global order extends further beyond the West, we now find political opposition, despite the extreme discontent it expresses, removed from any cultural or political purpose and labelled terrorist and evil. As opposition within the West becomes more desperate, those opposed to the IMF are being labelled terrorists. Moreover, as capitalism and science not only determine but actually represent material order, it is not possible to represent any 'rational' alternative to the current state of things or empirically defend any rationale for disturbing what is assumed to be the 'order' of nature. The clearest illustration of this is Dennett's perception of the 'ethics' of Darwinism:

> Those of us who lead fulfilling, even exciting, lives should hardly be shocked to see people in the disadvantaged world – and indeed in the drabber corners of our own world – turing to fanaticism of one brand or another. Would you settle docilely for a life of meaningless poverty, knowing what you know today about the world? The technology of the infosphere has recently made it conceivable for everybody on the globe to know what you know (with a lot of distortion). Until we can provide an environment for all people in which fanaticism doesn't make sense, we can expect more and more of it. But we don't have to accept it, and we don't have to respect it. Taking a few tips from Darwinian medicine, we can take steps to conserve what is valuable in every culture without keeping alive (or virulent) all its weaknesses. (Dennett 1995: 517)

As Dennett makes clear, there are no values in capitalist society, except for the economic. Nothing has 'meaning' but commerce and the 'free market'. Without any definitive ground to moral and ethical value, only the majority and ultimately might can determine what is right. In the light of the current battle against all and every 'brand' of political opposition to capital, the war against otherness was declared some time ago. The current wars against drugs and terror reveal the real conflict and suppression beneath capital's seemingly peaceful expansion. Furthermore, the brutality and cruelty we now see unleashed from within 'free society', where leaders freely gloat about killing conscripts and pushing refugees back out to sea, is a direct illustration of the fact that in the age of science and capital life itself no longer has any value.

As we are clearly witnessing, capitalism progresses by continually surmounting any obstacles that may confront it. Direct opposition only makes capitalism stronger. Because capitalism is material order, the economists, as with the scientists, have all the 'reasons'. As any 'alternative' to either capitalism or science is beyond representation, opposition cannot be represented or debated, as any other to the present state of things can only be based on idealism. In line with this, Marx conceived opposition to capital to derive not from 'ideology' but disaffection, and class conflict to be driven, not by opposing ideals but a conflict of natures.

Marx's concept of value ultimately derives from what he recognized to be the creative potential of activity. Value, in this respect, is seen to be intrinsic to the relation between producer and produced as it arises solely within the continuity in which an object is made. Although difference in value is said to be incapable of being exchanged in kind or quantified, in the wage-relation, where the worker is payed a sum less than the object's exchange value, the creative potential of activity serves as the origin of 'surplus value' and, ultimately, capital. Marx argued, from this perspective, that the commodification of labour ends up turning the worker's creative capacity into the source of their own domination. The exchange of labour time for wages becomes necessary for existence, but material life is deprived of any intrinsic value for the worker, being a machine simply in the service of capital itself. As capital seeks to exploit ever more value from labour, the worker and the capitalist struggle over the value of time. Marx predicted that the more capital dominated material existence, the greater the sense of alienation felt by the worker. Finally, the collective sense of alienation was expected to give rise to a revolutionary consciousness where a united working class would create a new order where potential would not be separated from life.

Today, in spite of the much publicized 'anti-capitalist' protest, alienation is more in decline than a revolutionary force. Despite the many gains made by workers in the struggle for better working conditions, wage-earners have failed to unite either as a class or in opposition to capital. From another perspective, however, there seems to be some truth in Marx's account of capitalism's elision of creativity and 'value'. The spread of commodification and the capitalist mode of production is rapidly destroying every 'aesthetic' quality. Art is now nothing more than a form of entertainment. Harold Bloom's cannon has been completely pillaged by the cinema industry, which has stripped literature of everything but plot and suspense. Every one of the 'muses', has become nothing more than a source of amusement. The same goes for culture which, once commodified, is removed from history and reduced to an object of consumption. With all production based purely on profit, and all modes of exchange now quantified, art and culture have become reduced to representations of themselves.

Along with the destruction of art the creative moniker is now shifting towards the traditionally more 'intellectual' discourses. New technologies, wonder drugs and varieties of fruit are today the result of 'creative science'. Advertisers and entrepreneurs are now the ones who have 'ideas', while software developers are now the model of the 'temperamental artistic types'. In the meantime, artists have been confined to producing attractive designs, catchy tunes or exciting plots and narratives. Having been appropriated by capital, art on the whole has been transformed from a mode of aesthetic production into the 'entertainment industry', where music, film, fine art, etc. are 'manufactured'.

Science further complements capital's suppression of creativity with the reduction of change to chance and chaos. An ever-growing number of disciplines, from neuroscience and artificial intelligence to neo-Darwinist social theory are trying their hardest to reduce human creativity, artistic or otherwise, to a combination of intelligence, skill and luck. In as good as every case the brain is reduced to some form of complex parallel computer, thereby limiting thought in its entirety to the form of mechanism and creativity to either chance or the engineering of possibilities. In typical fashion, Dennett informs us the works of Beethoven can be attributed to the combination of having the right set of genes for mastering the piano, being born into a musical household and throwing together the odd set of notes (Dennett 1995). This random distribution of genes and 'memes', together with the selective power of the market, is said to constitute the foundation of all social production.

As Dennett clearly exemplifies, the current predominance of scientific thought has arisen at the expense of any sense of 'creativity'. The problem is that arguments like the above cannot be argued against because the only basis to 'aesthetic' difference is sensibility itself. Simply put, only those who 'get it', or intuit the manner in which differences are apprehended or produced can conceive how and why creativity cannot be reduced to either materiality or chance. Sadly, however, as objective life becomes ever more materialized, sensibility in general is becoming increasingly substanceless where all forms of aesthetic difference are exchanged for an indifferent pleasure. In all, we are losing touch with creativity itself.

The fact that the destruction of culture parallels the decline of political consciousness tells us that Marx's concept of value is not so much a limitation but a limit. Although difference is without doubt intrinsic to the relation between subject and object, creativity does not derive from the individual alone. Value, culture or aesthetic difference resides solely in the duration or 'life' of culture and the relations that unfold within it. The origin of difference is comparable to the 'substance' of sensibility. Accordingly, the more life is commodified, and relations quantified, the more the value of culture declines and sensibility is stripped of its substance. Unfortunately, as we can now see, the more we are deprived of difference and the substance of life is destroyed, the less 'conscious' we are of change and the nature of existence. The only way we can have insight into the nature of capital and science is to extend our understanding of the production and nature of difference. As such a project is by nature beyond the limits of empiricism and representation, metaphysics emerges as the ultimate basis of politics. We can no longer wait for the revolution to come, as Marx thought, and many, including Hardt and Negri, still believe.

DIFFERENCE AND SENSIBILITY

If we could exclude every functional, material and formal attribute of human desire, the only thing we would find remaining is its affective expression and apprehension. For instance, it is not different foods we desire, as opposed to need, but differences in taste. We can say, for this reason, that the object of human desire, and that which distinguishes it from need, is the apprehension of its expression. The clearest illustration of this is human sexuality, where apprehension has become an end in itself, qualitatively distinct from procreation. Sex, however, is in no way the motor of desire as a whole. Broadly speaking, the nature of human desire can be seen to derive from the emergence of affective self-awareness. Through the evolution of consciousness we have acquired the additional capacity for apprehending differences in apprehension itself.

If action was motivated solely by need then we would expect the human, as with the rest of the animal species, to be content and certainly more stable with a given set of necessities. If all we required in life was warm clothing, comfortable lodgings, a well-balanced diet and suitable partner then the difficulties we could expect to face would not go beyond the likes of efficacy and supply. In contrast to this, history reveals that for all time and in every culture difference has been integral to human activity in general. Instead of sticking to water to quench our thirst, for example, we have created teas, beverages, juices and wines, etc. Rather than constructing purely functional shelters, we have developed architecture. We do not wear clothes solely to keep warm, but also for how they look. In addition to providing a means to communicate information, language has created the potential for literature, poetry and humour, etc. etc.

Just as difference adds an aesthetic dimension to need, sensibility, or the awareness of affective change, can be seen to add an aesthetic dimension to the evolution of form and function. Following the emergence of consciousness, the evolutionary process has become 'intensive' as well as extensive. Although, most notably with music, differences are produced solely for apprehension itself, the desire for difference transcends any distinction between 'art' and function. Although, as Kant has argued, there can be no 'objective' grounds for determining matters of taste, sensibility cannot be removed from sensation. As sensibility determines the apprehension of all differences the bourgeois distinction between art and culture is essentially undermined.

Whether difference is created for apprehension alone or in relation to need, both the motivation and the means remain the same. Moreover, the impetus to create not only new forms of art, cuisine and music but equally new social and sexual relations, gestures, types of speech and ways to relax, as well as think, is, in Spinoza's terminology, *causa sui* or cause of itself. We cannot say, for instance, that desire is ultimately motivated towards pleasure simply because difference is itself 'affective'. That is, it is not for the indifference of pleasure that we desire new types of wine or music but the differences in our affective apprehension of them. As the cultural and historical ubiquity of music is testament, there is no reason, purpose or goal for creating differences other than creativity itself.

The likes of cuisine, dress, architecture and sexuality demonstrate that sensibility has added an aesthetic dimension to the more practical needs addressed by the intellect. Because affectivity is apprehended solely in the continuity of duration, aesthetic differences have been integrated into almost every form of human practice. Cuisine, for example, as opposed to 'food', represents the blending of available produce, farming practices, social rituals, nutritional needs and so on within the sensibilities of taste. Moreover, not only does the desire for change and difference within taste have an effect on the ways in which foods are prepared, it in turn influences the desire for particular types of produce and the nature of farming practices, etc. Broadly speaking, sensibility constitutes a sort of temporal surface expressing the manifold desires that bind practices to their material componentry.

As Bergson demonstrates in *Time and Free Will*, the duration of sensibility is comprised of a multiplicity of affective states that are apprehended as interpenetrating and qualitatively distinct. Affectivity, in this sense, provides a means of conceiving differences that are not spatially determined and multiplicities that are neither numerical nor a multiple of the one. The 'unity' of sensibility when apprehended in its duration, and not from the numerical unity of reflective consciousness, is its multiplicity. Since it is through sensibility that the immanent relations between self, others and the environment are expressed and the aesthetic relation between desire and habitat is maintained, cultural difference is, as with affectivity, a qualitative multiplicity. Although cultures may be numerically multiple, as well as spatially unified, cultural difference in itself is manifest in the manifold desires and interrelated practices enfolded in the material composition of the social and its environment. Accordingly, culture exists nowhere else but in time, in the continuity of its duration – giving, amongst other things, substance to sensibility and aesthetics to practice.

The unity of reflective consciousness and the spatial framework that determines objectivity are in themselves qualitatively distinct from the manifold affects that make up sensibility. This radical distinction may contribute to the appearance of their being separated but because all qualitative differences reside within sensibility reflective consciousness can be equally regarded as one of its constituents – just as the intellect presents but an aspect of consciousness as well as the mind. It is in this sense that sensibility is, for example, enfolded within the spatial framework of reflective consciousness which not only unites objectivity with desire but adds an aesthetic dimension to perception as a whole.

In *Time and Free Will* Bergson reveals how the form of representation has created the illusion that differences in apprehension are caused directly by an object's material qualities. As expressions such as the 'scent of a rose' and the 'taste of wine' clearly illustrate, sensations are not named in themselves but according to the objects with which they correspond. As a consequence, representation gives rise to the impression that one can represent differences that can only be apprehended simply by representing the object itself. In contrast to this, introspection will reveal that no manner of taste is either constant or not to some degree acquired. The coffee I enjoy now, for instance, was despised in youth, is unpleasant with certain foods nor prepared to the liking of my Turkish neighbour. Not only does our own 'taste' continually vary, therefore, the same object will taste differently to others.

Variations in our own and others apprehension of the same object, reveal sensation to be inseparable from sensibility. While the flavour of coffee may derive from its material qualities, the 'taste' will vary according to the combined effects of past experience and one's present state of being. The illusion, in this case, lies not in the sensation but the idea of an independent object embodying the 'flavour of coffee'. Not only has the material form of coffee continually evolved, its evolution is inseparable from the variation of cultural, regional and individual sensibilities that it parallels.

Revealing more than just flavour, the taste of coffee is at once an expression of its desirability. Taste, as with all other modes of apprehension, expresses, by way of intensity, the level of our attraction or aversion to the thing. Even though in language we invariably say that we 'like the taste', thereby implying that it is the sensation that is evaluated, attraction is in fact inseparable from the immediacy or duration of apprehension itself. The taste of the wine for this reason expresses our evaluation and our apprehension of its qualities at the same time. It is the taste of the coffee, the look of the face or the smell of the rose, etc. that reveals the nature of our attraction.

Broadly speaking, affectivity can be regarded as the expression, in positive or negative differences in intensity, of how much we desire to repeat an encounter with someone or something. Conversely, it can just as easily be said that we are attracted to whatever affects us positively. It is important, however, not to confuse affect with effect, as the two are radically distinct. Although one's first cigarette may have produced rather unpleasant *effects*, it was most probably the way in which one was *affected* that determined if and when there was to be a next one. The immediacy of apprehension, in other words, not only expresses desirability but is, at the same time, its evaluation – we find someone attractive, for instance, because they 'look' good. And as attraction and aversion are both solely intensive, the only grounds for evaluating desirability are ultimately the evaluation itself.

Prior to having tasted it, one's idea of coffee will largely conform to what the name denotes – the abstract set or empty class of the thing in general. Following an initial encounter, in addition to gaining an idea of the flavour of coffee, it may eventually become an 'acquired taste'. In the process, it is not that one grows to like the taste, it is the sensation itself that changes from one of disgust to something desired. One could argue that through repetition the senses grow used to the flavour and smell, but opposing the nature of habit we find that repeating the same will eventually and invariably lead to boredom — one would just as quickly become sick of the taste if once acquired it did not vary. As the acquiring and dispensing of taste both illustrate, it is neither ideas nor habits that condition the immediate apprehension of things, but the state of one's desire.

If, for example, we have the good fortune to taste an exceptional bottle of wine, we will invariably find that the cheap claret we ordinarily drink will never taste quite the same. As this demonstrates, the manner in which something affects us expresses not so much the form of our sensibility but the event of its transformation. Furthermore, although the wine that we find to be outstanding differs from what we are used to, its difference does not derive from contrast but is given in its actual taste. This is further illustrated by what happens when we return to what we usually drink, for we will notice that it no longer tastes as good, or at least the same, as it did. Hence, it is not the wine that has changed but ourselves, for the difference between before and after derives from our sensibility.

As Bergson has demonstrated, neither desire nor sensibility conform to the structure of the objective world. Rather than a set of discrete individual wants and needs, desires and affections are by nature manifold and interpenetrating. The singular taste of a glass of wine, for instance, is comprised of what Bergson terms a 'qualitative multiplicity' of distinct although inseparable sensations. Although singular in its apprehension, the taste itself has no unified sense other than its multiplicity. In addition to differences in perception, sensibility also expresses a multiplicity of singular although interrelated desires. The way in which we are affected by certain foods, for instance, may relate simply to the need for energy and hunger, or it may concern nutrition and express our physical well-being, alternatively, it may be in relation to taste, thereby expressing our social place and history, or it may be a cause of anxiety, etc. etc. Ordinarily our response to an object or situation will concern a number of different though inseparable desires. And just as the dinner menu can greatly affect the taste of the wine, our manifold desires are continuously influencing each other – with the condition of the self and the paths it follows in life being expressed in its multiple affections rather than any unified direction or state.

Although we will probably be able to recall only the more significant events in our lives, desire and – as a consequence – sensibility change with every encounter. Sensibility is composed of an unbroken succession of manifold affects, each of which expresses a change in the form of desire. As Bergson demonstrates in *Matter and Memory*, the enduring sense of how we have been affected by something constitutes what he terms a 'pure' or virtual memory. Rather than a memory *of* the past, the pure memory or sense of past affects subsists within the duration of the present. From this perspective we find that our ordinary conceptions of the past and present are inverted: while the present is that which is always passing, the past is that which never passes. And although this may sound somewhat counter-intuitive, it is quite straightforward – for there is nowhere else that the past can endure than in the duration of the living. It is the past that composes our current disposition.

> [E]ven though we may have no distinct idea of it, we feel vaguely that our past remains present to us. What are we, in fact, what is our *character*, if not the condensation of the history that we have lived from our birth – nay, even before our birth, since we bring with us prenatal dispositions? Doubtless we think with only a small part of our past, but it is with our entire past, including the original bent of our soul, that we desire, will and act. (Bergson 1983: 5)

The past, in this sense, is not a sum of individual memories, but a fluid, interpenetrating and continuously changing multiplicity of past affects. For instance, although we may have forgotten what we were taught at school, how we were taught, and how we were affected by the teaching we received, remains inseparable from our sensibilities. In subjective terms, pure memory is comparable to the infinitive of disposition or that part of one's character that can only be enacted. Generally speaking, it is the continuity of memory that constitutes the substance of one's 'nature': determining the manifold characteristics of sensibility and governing the inclinations of desire.

Because the duration within which life unfolds is as indivisible as substance itself, the individual is situated within a continuum of changing relations and a present which has always been and has never been past. From this perspective, the continuity of memory can also be seen to transcend the individual in both space and time, tying their sensibility and desire to the movements and gestures of others, the composition of the environment and a history exceeding their own duration. And it is this immanent and transcendent memory that contains the differences constitutive of cultures and collectives of any kind. Culture, in the widest sense of the term, therefore resides not in given practices or the material composition of the subject and his or her milieu, but the integrated movement and transformation of the 'whole'. It is the continuous or 'virtual' element of cultural difference which constitutes the 'substance' of sensibility, determining the nature of our attractions, indifferences, aversions and inclinations.

Just as our apprehension of something is not wholly attributable to the object itself, the memory of how we are affected is not entirely contained in the 'material' brain. The pure memory coexisting and composing the living self, occupies the duration or life of the mind. Neither, strictly speaking, corporeal nor incorporeal, it is the absolute *mobilité* of the self that constitutes the 'substance' of sensibility. Even though apprehension exceeds the object encountered, the fact that it transforms our desire means that the individual and his or her environment evolve in tandem. Broadly speaking we can say that from within the continuity of duration, changes in sensibility parallel the transformation of the equally substantial environment. Moreover, from this perspective, it is the addition of memory that differentiates the self and the world.

Because the past endures within our present disposition, we cannot encounter even the same thing twice without our apprehension of it changing. Each time we listen to a piece of music, for instance, we hear it differently. Although a song will occasionally improve or 'grow on us' through repetition, it usually and in time inevitably results in either boredom or, in many cases, extreme aversion. As many of today's advertising campaigns clearly illustrate, although some music requires numerous listenings to be fully appreciated, enough repetition will turn even the finest in classical music into a cause of suffering. In line with this, it is difference and repetition that ultimately remain as the essential attributes of discernment.

POLITICAL DESIRES

As Bergson further demonstrates, ideas such as choice and free will betray an inherent inconsistency, for if the will is to determine an act, the mind must be 'ahead' of the body's duration (Bergson 1919: 181). Since mind and body coexist, subject and object, idea and act cannot be distinguished. Instead of determining the future, choice is fundamentally retrospective, as it is only ever made after an action is 'completed' and it is only in 'retrospect' that the mind gains ascendancy over the body. The idea of choice, as Mill describes it, presupposes at least two distinct and equal possibilities and a mind free to decide between them. However, as Bergson points out, the mind cannot be distinguished from sensibility and desire, and no decision is ever free from inclination. Rather than choice, an action is itself a decision to follow the pull of desire or not. Our only alternative in life is either to follow our desires or repress them.

Contrary to this, the prevailing belief is that smoking, pregnancy, sexuality, drug use, career, poverty and unemployment are all pursuits one freely chooses. At what point, however, can we say that we chose our path in life, or that we chose to be an accountant, lawyer, junkie, straight, gay or into techno? If such things were truly chosen then we would expect to find all straight people to have chosen *not* to be gay or take drugs and so on. On the other hand, it is because reflective thought and sensibility are qualitatively distinct that they appear to be removed from one another. Within the continuity in which one thinks and acts the mind is not only inseparable from sensibility and action but endures in tandem with the will, precluding the 'spatial' separation that would allow the mind to determine the body to act. The abstract and detached perspective assumed by the liberal subject is inescapably alloyed with affectivity, emotion and desire, infecting its universality with difference and undermining its objectivity with the continuous presence of inclination and desire.

Rather than intentional, in this respect, the continuity of thought and action is 'intensional' – where desire is expressed by the multiplicity of affects manifest within sensibility. It is not that thought and action do not contain distinct elements, but that within continuity they are inseparable from the continuity of desire and affectivity. Rather than the enactment of a series of discrete actions, in this sense, the process of getting out of bed, making the coffee, preparing the porridge, etc. is governed by a continuous succession of affective states. As Bergson writes:

> The duration *wherein we see ourselves acting*, and in which it is useful that we should see ourselves, is a duration whose elements are dissociated and juxtaposed. The duration *wherein we act* is a duration wherein our states melt into each other. (Bergson 1991: 186)

One's own experience will show that, aside from when reflecting on philosophical problems, the greater part of our lives unfold within the duration '*wherein we act*' rather than '*see ourselves acting*'. We are, for this reason, largely unaware of the fact that the composition of our lives and our sensibilities are continuously changing. Television footage of our recent past, for example, reveals how much our tastes can transform over relatively short periods of time. Although somewhat arbitrary time-frames, the 'eighties', 'seventies' and 'sixties', etc. demonstrate not only a continuous change in taste but the fact that sensibility traverses the population as a whole. The seventies are a clear illustration of how the 'aesthetic' of the age affected everyone – as historical evidence now shows, flared trousers, loud ties and prominent sideburns were the norm. Consequently, no one can be said to have had complete control in 'choosing' to look the way they did.

What horrifies many who look back on the seventies is not so much the look of what they used to wear but the fact they desired to wear it. As such examples show, it is more accurate to say that it is we who are within desire and desire that chooses us, rather than the other way round. While the reflective self has some power in deciding whether or not to act upon them, it is not we who determine the nature of our likes and dislikes. Although many are forced to choose between keeping up appearances or 'coming out', one does not 'choose' to be attracted to members of one's own sex. In every case we 'find' ourselves within desire, just as one finds oneself to be gay or straight, or in between, or interested in sport, art, cooking or astrophysics. Moreover, it is desire that binds the subject to actuality. Every aspect of the objective world – from the language and gestures of urban youth, the colour of cars or bed-linen, to the structure of the universe – is accompanied by a category of desire. And although, for example, one may be forced to do things that are of no interest, have no means of realizing certain desires or simply have a sense of something missing, it is the multiplicity of desires, inherent to the duration 'wherein we act', that make up the substance of the living self.

As that which endures in the continuity of desire, giving substance and direction to our likes and dislikes, the 'virtual' memory of the past gives depth to the duration of thought and action. Just as ideas for the creation of cuisines, fine art and music emerge within sensibility, guiding the composition of tastes, colours and sounds, daily life is governed by a constantly varying multiplicity of affective inclinations which, in turn, direct the continuity of thought and action. And as within duration objectivity in general becomes an indivisible continuum, itself infected with the continuity of affective variation, others and objects are transformed into movements and singularities. Which is equally the case with the objective self, its actions and ideas. Although the content of thought, for example, appears to unfold as a series of discrete linguistic elements, it does so not in a vacuum but within the indivisible duration of sensibility. And as within the continuity of duration language is inseparable from affectivity, thought itself must be seen as an indivisible process where the discrete units of language become what Bergson terms 'partial expressions' of a continuously changing composition.

As the characteristics of representation condition all facets of the commodity, then in addition to objective form, commodification can be seen to bring about the materialization of cultural differences. Through the process of commodification, 'cultures' are reduced to their material elements and practices and divorced from the milieu within which they evolve. Rather than serving as catalysts for multiculturalism, for instance, today's 'world music', 'ethnic cuisine' and 'indigenous arts' transform their contents into static representations of abstract and undifferentiated Western categories. Whereas Indian cuisine has evolved over thousands of years, integrating environmental conditions, modes of practice, religious beliefs and centuries of migration, conquest and colonization within the singularity of its people's living sensibilities, commercialization has reduced it either to the stereotypical curry or recipes for combining the necessary spices. As a consequence, difference is frozen in material form. As we are currently witnessing with the growth of global tourism, representation is progressively taking the place of reality. This exact transformation is occurring across the spectrum of contemporary capitalist existence, confining everything from food to fashion and music to human identity itself solely to its material composition.

Commodification can be seen to reduce difference to its lowest common denominator. Everything, from cuisine to music, has lost all 'substance' in recent years, just as a hamburger fulfils the general requirements of taste, music, film and television come to fill the vacuum of time with repetition for its own sake. As commodification negates the difference of history, we find that not only aesthetic sense but also social sensibilities of all kinds are in decline. On the one hand, the current movement of change is destroying the wisdom and difference that gives continuity to culture and change. On the other hand, the 'difference' of culture and life in general continues in the ongoing resistance and reluctance of cultures to what Harry Cleaver refers to as the 'imposition' of work (Cleaver 1979). With virtually every culture and people that has been colonized or enslaved by capital, the memory of the past continues in the affective distaste with the cultural vacuum of capitalist existence. Beneath the 'autonomy' of struggle, therefore, it is now possible to conceive the multiplicity of difference and the duration of culture.

As capital and science continue the general tendency towards turning ourselves and the globe into an integrated and self-governing mechanism, the modern subject is becoming increasingly individuated. With television, the telephone and the Internet, private car and home and individual work contract, the individual is becoming a world unto himself. Not only is the individual distanced from others by technology, but he or she is denied anything other than 'quantitative' relations with all but an increasing few by the ubiquity of the monetary exchange relation. The more everything becomes commodified and individuated, the more 'culture' and aesthetic relations in general are deprived of continuity and substance. It is not surprising, therefore, to find capitalism most advanced in the new colonies, which are, to varying degrees, all born out of the spirit of *terra nullius* as much as is Australia. With the conquest of the indigenous population, the colonizers were free to exploit the resources and industrial material of their respective continents.

Although for the most part less brutal, the spread of free enterprise and exploitation is an ongoing process. With the global enforcement of free market policies and deregulation, science, capitalism and democracy are advancing the unified human machine to all corners of the globe. Given the enormous potential benefits that come with capital and the general willingness to accept material wealth, capitalism has for the greater part spread relatively unhindered. In the process, however, we now find that culture as much as nature is coming under threat. Because culture resides not only in the material elements and practices of its peoples but in the movement of cultural sensibility itself, commodification and individuation have the effect of eliding cultural continuity and practice. The purely material and mechanistic nature of capitalism means that it is intrinsically antithetical to cultural difference.

As any form of cultural practice, as much as so-called state communism, cannot become capitalist without becoming other than itself, an ever increasing antagonism is growing between those who wish to defend their cultures and the power-brokers of capitalist expansion. The sad truth, however, is that capitalism will eventually break down any obstacle to itself, if not by blowing it up then turning it into a source of revenue: for example, tourism and cheap labour.

The inevitable demise of political opposition to, as well as cultural production within, capital is best illustrated by the so-called era of postmodernity. The advent of the postmodern effectively means the dissolution of every civil rights, political and artistic movement to have grown out of the West. Although the state went to great lengths to effect such a goal, the main cause of the demise of politics and art in the West has been the combined forces of individuation and commodification. Once money became the dominating principle of the art market, one had to compete to survive and with the death of all and every 'movement' the history of art became open to reproduction. Similarly, on the political front, the new economic reality meant that getting a job and staying afloat was enough of a battle for any individual.

Although capitalism is only the economic aspect of the broad tendency that is transforming the globe, and within this tendency every aspect of material need is being addressed in some way, the one thing that cannot be satisfied is the nature of desire. With the elision of the substance of cultural and aesthetic difference it appears we are also losing the substance of our sensibilities. Sensibility, in this sense, is what integrates us with the movement of material change, and coordinates our actions and reactions with others and differentiates our material environment. Within capitalism, however, sensibility is devoid of substance. As a consequence, time needs to be constantly filled with the pressures of work and life as well and entertained by the never-ending narratives of film and television.

It is becoming apparent that for an ever increasing number of people, work and entertainment are not enough to fill the vacuum of existence. The fastest growing afflictions today are boredom and depression. While one expresses positively the desire for something more, the other is a clear statement on how lacking in substance contemporary life has become. In one sense, as duration is being stripped of substance, time itself is becoming a problem – not for the understanding but for sensibility. The prevalence of boredom today clearly indicates that giving substance to time is possibly of greater importance than having everything one needs.

Depression, on the other hand, is the disease of capitalism. It is the pure expression of desire without substance and sensibility with no potential. Religion and spirituality have become so devoid of substance they only resonate the vacuum. Science is constantly producing chemical solutions and therapy has turned the need for friendship into a source of profit.

The primary means through which sensibility manages to acquire substance is through drugs. The rapid rise in levels of addiction can be seen as a means of escaping a life of mechanical repetition. The massive rise in cocaine and heroin use in the past decades represents nothing less than the desire to give 'substance' to sensibility. Drugs, in this sense are a means of survival for an increasing number. The nature of aesthetics and difference itself tells us that drug addiction is not a cure but a stopgap. And, just as the war on terror is the means whereby capitalist order is able to combat any and all external differences, the war on drugs is the means by which order is maintained from within. Sanctioned by the groundless charge of criminality, millions upon millions of 'minorities', for instance, are being imprisoned and denied cultural and political power.

The primary fault of the current movement of things is that human order is just as incommensurate with the nature of human desire as it is with the order of nature. Just as straight lines and mechanical order contrast with the composition of nature and a face-lift doesn't quite match the natural composition of the face, so it is that material society doesn't fit with the composition of change. Nature, however, does not mean untouched, it signifies the logic of change and continuity. Culture, also, does not mean ways and peoples of the past but the implication of the past within the desires and practices of the present. If we are to change the direction of things, this will not be achieved solely through direct opposition to either capitalism or science but by working out how we can avoid making economics and our knowledge of the material world ends in themselves.

In this regard, the logic of aesthetic difference provides the basis of a truly 'evolutionary' ethics, for it represents continuity through change and difference in itself rather than from others. If we are to change the nature of existence, however, it will not be through some proletariat revolution, but only through the revaluation of thought and values. If we are to escape the movement of capitalism and the destruction of aesthetic, cultural and environmental relations, then we must give value to the unquantifiable qualities that give substance and continuity to cultural difference and sensibility. The aim of any future politics must not be to oppose capital, science or democracy but to make culture not commodities the basis of difference, substance not matter the basis of practice and desire not choice the basis of ethics and politics.

In Deleuze's words, the equation of difference and repetition forms the foundation, not only of aesthetic production but of ethics. The productive relations or common notions transcending subject and object are what ultimately distinguish the ethics of desire from liberal freedom. It is by creating differences in what we are attracted to, or part of, that we maintain the substance of culture and give momentum to movement. And it is through desire that we respond to the ongoing problems posed by life and change. Aesthetics and ethics, in this sense, share the same logic, as their value derives from the degree to which different responses to the problem of repetition maintain the continuity of that which differentiates repetition itself.

With the current capitalist social order and the pathologization of anything that conflicts with its routine, we find the problems of existence continually pushed to the margin and confined. Although all 'desires' are obviously not ethical, solving life's problems through the law alone leads only to the inevitable repetition of transgression. On the one hand, the law requires transgession in order to function. On the other, repression turns transgression itself into the basis of desire. While the law, as with money and science, will always have a function, as abuses of power will undoubtedly remain, it is only by, paradoxically, giving freedom to desire that we will be able to find solutions to problems that desire itself manifests.

As Bergson has suggested, it is up to philosophy to 'reverse the habits of thought'. This, however, is more than simply a problem of epistemology, for the habits of thought are responsible for the current state of things. This 'reversal' does not require the revival of specific cultural questions or a return to 'nature', but rather giving life to thought. Traditional practices, artistic movements and 'nature' in this respect do not so much constitute objects as modes of a productive and differential logic. In this sense, if we are to avoid expending our environment, we must shift the basis of practice from matter to substance, rather than return to pre-industrial times. Similarly, if we are to escape the current decline into ineptitude and banality we must make aesthetic difference the basis of value rather than mechanical repetition.

Bibliography

This bibliography includes works cited within the text, as well as additional material consulted during the course of its writing.

Agamben, Giorgio, 1993a. *The Coming Community*, trans. Michael Hardt. Minneapolis, MN: University of Minnesota Press.

——, 1993b. *Infancy and History: Essays on the Destruction of Experience*, trans. Liz Heron. London and New York: Verso.

Alliez, Eric, 1996. *Capital Times*, trans. Georges van den Abbeele. Minneapolis, MN: University of Minnesota Press.

Anderson, Alan Ross (ed.), 1964. *Minds and Machines*. New Jersey: Prentice-Hall.

Ansell Pearson, Keith, 1997. *Viroid Life: Perspectives on Nietzsche and the Transhuman Condition*. London and New York: Routledge.

——, 1999. *Germinal Life: The Difference and Repetition of Deleuze*. London and New York: Routledge.

——, (ed.), 1997. *Deleuze and Philosophy: The Difference Engineer*. London: Routledge.

Arendt, Hannah, 1978. *The Life of the Mind*. San Diego, CA: Harcourt Brace.

Aristotle, 1966. *Metaphysics*, trans. Hippocrates G. Apostle. Bloomington, IN, and London: Indiana University Press.

——, 1976. *Ethics*, trans. J. A. K. Thompson. London: Penguin.

——, 1981. *The Politics*, trans. T. A. Sinclair. London: Penguin.

——, 1996. *Physics*, trans. Robin Waterfield. Oxford: Oxford University Press.

Baldwin, James Mark, 1896. 'A New Factor in Evolution', *American Naturalist*, 30: 441–51, 536–53.

Balibar, Etienne, 1995. *The Philosophy of Marx*, trans. Chris Turner. London and New York: Verso.

——, 1998. *Spinoza and Politics*, trans. Peter Snowdon. London: Verso.

Bergson, Henri, 1919. *Time and Free Will*, trans. F. L. Pogson. New York: Macmillan. (Originally published as *Essai sur les données immédiates de la conscience*. Paris: Presses Universitaires de France, 1889.)

——, 1920. *Mind-Energy*, trans. H. Wildon Carr. London: MacMillan. (Originally published as *L'Energie spirituelle*. Paris: Presses Universitaires de France, 1919.)

——, 1949. 'Quid Aristoteles de loco senserit', French trans. R. M. Mossé-Bastide in *Les Etudes Bergsoniennes*, 2: 27–104. (Original in Latin, 1889.)

——, 1965. *Duration and Simultaneity*, trans. Leon Jacobson. Indianapolis, IN: Bobbs-Merrill. (Originally published as *Durée et simultanéité*. Paris: Presses Universitaires de France, 1922.)

——, 1972. *Mélanges*. Paris: Presses Universitaires de France.

——, 1977. *The Two Sources of Morality and Religion*, trans. Cloudesley Brereton and R. Ashley Audra. Notre Dame, IN: University of Notre Dame Press. (Originally published as *Les deux Sources de la morale et de la religion*. Paris: Presses Universitaires de France, 1932.)

——, 1983. *Creative Evolution*, trans. Arthur Mitchell. Lanham: University Press of America. (Originally published as *L'Evolution créatrice*. Paris: Presses Universitaires de France, 1907.)

——, 1991. *Matter and Memory*, trans. N. M. Paul and W. S. Palmer. New York: Zone Books. (Originally published as *Matière et mémoire*. Paris: Presses Universitaires de France, 1896.)

——, 1992. *The Creative Mind*, trans. Mabelle L. Andison. New York: First Carol Publishing. (Originally published as *La Pensée et le mouvant*. Paris: Presses Universitaires de France, 1934.)

Bohm, David, 1980. *Wholeness and the Implicate Order*. London: Routledge.

——, 1986. 'Time, the Implicate Order, and Pre-Space', in Griffen (ed.) 1986, pp. 177–208.

Boundas, Constantin V., 1996. 'Deleuze–Bergson: An Ontology of the Virtual', in Patton (ed.), 1996, pp. 81–106.

——, 1997. 'Deleuze on Time and Memory', *Antithesis*, 8 (2): pp. 11–29.

Boyer, Carl B., 1949. *The History of the Calculus and its Conceptual Development*. New York: Dover Publications.

Broglie, Louis de, 1969. *Physics and Microphysics*, trans. Martin Davidson. London: Hutchinson.

Brouwer, L. E. J., 1913. 'Intuitionism and Formalism', in *L. E. J. Brouwer. Collected Works: Volume One: Philosophy and Foundations of Mathematics*. A. Heyting (ed.), Amsterdam: New Holland, 1975, pp. 123–38.

Cantor, Georg, 1883. 'Foundations of a General Theory of Manifolds: A Mathematical–Philosophical Study in the Theory of the Infinite', trans. Uwe Parpart. *The Campaigner: The Theoretical Journal of the National Caucus of Labour Committees*, 9 (1976): 69–96.

——, 1899. 'Letter to Dedekind', in *From Frege to Gödel*. Jean van Heijencourt (ed.), Cambridge, MA: Harvard University Press, 1967, pp. 113–17.

Capek, Milic, 1971. *Bergson and Modern Physics*. Dordrecht: D. Reidel.

Cleaver, Harry, 1979. *Reading* Capital *Politically*. Brighton: Harvester Press.

Coveney, Peter and Highfield, Roger, 1996. *Frontiers of Complexity*. London: Faber & Faber.

Csányi, V. and Kampis, G., 1985. 'Autogenesis: The Evolution of Replicative Systems', *Journal of Theoretical Biology*, 114: 303–21.

Curley, Edwin, 1969. *Spinoza's Metaphysics*. Cambridge: Harvard University Press.

——, 1988. *Behind the Geometrical Method: A Reading of Spinoza's Ethics*. Princeton, NJ: Princeton University Press.

Darwin, Charles, 1993. *The Origin of Species*. New York: Random House.

Dauben, Joseph Warren, 1979. *Georg Cantor: His Mathematics and Philosophy of the Infinite*. Cambridge, MA, and London: Harvard University Press.

Davies, Paul and Gribbin, John, 1992. *The Matter Myth: Beyond Chaos and Complexity*. London: Penguin.

Davis, Martin (ed.), 1965. *The Undecidable*. Hewlett, New York: Raven Press.

Dawkins, Richard, 1986. *The Blind Watchmaker*. New York: W. W. Norton.

Deleuze, Gilles, 1956. 'La Conception de la différence chez Bergson', in *Les Etudes Bergsoniennes*, 4: 77–112.

——, 1984. *Kant's Critical Philosophy*, trans. Hugh Tomlinson and Barbara Habberjam. London: The Athlone Press.

——, 1986. *Cinema 1: The Movement-Image*, trans. Hugh Tomlinson and Barbara Habberjam. London: The Athlone Press.

——, 1988. *Spinoza: Practical Philosophy*, trans. Robert Hurley. San Francisco, CA: City Lights Books.

——, 1989. *Cinema 2: The Time-Image*, trans. Hugh Tomlinson and Robert Gelata. Minneapolis, MN: University of Minnesota Press.

——, 1990. *The Logic of Sense*, trans. Mark Lester with Charles Stivale, ed. Constantin Boundas. New York: Columbia University Press.

——, 1991. *Bergsonism*, trans. Hugh Tomlinson and Barbara Habberjam. New York: Zone Books.

——, 1992. *Expressionism in Philosophy: Spinoza*, trans. Martin Joughin. New York: Zone Books.

——, 1993. *The Fold: Leibniz and the Baroque*, trans. Tom Conley. London: The Athlone Press.

——, 1994. *Difference and Repetition*, trans. Paul Patton. New York: Columbia University Press.

Deleuze, Gilles and Guattari, Felix, 1983. *Anti-Oedipus*, trans. Robert Hurley, Mark Seem and Helen R. Lane. Minneapolis, MN: University of Minnesota Press.

——, 1987. *A Thousand Plateaus*, trans. Brian Massumi. Minneapolis, MN: University of Minnesota Press.

——, 1994. *What is Philosophy?*, trans. Hugh Tomlinson and Graham Burchell. New York: Columbia University Press.

Dennett, Daniel C., 1995. *Darwin's Dangerous Idea*. London: Penguin.

Derrida, Jacques, 1982. *Margins of Philosophy*, trans. Alan Bass. Hemel Hempstead: Harvester–Wheatsheaf.

Eldredge, Niles and Gould, Stephen Jay, 1972. 'Punctuated Equilibria: An Alternative to Phyletic Gradualism', in Thomas J. M. Schopf (ed.), *Models in Paleobiology*. San Francisco: Freeman, Cooper & Co., pp. 82–115.

Foucault, Michel, 1980. *Power/Knowledge*, ed. Colin Gordon. New York: Pantheon.

Frege, Gottlob, 1950. *The Foundations of Arithmetic*, trans. J. L. Austin. Oxford: Basil Blackwell.

Gandy, Robin, 1988. 'The Confluence of Ideas in 1936', in Herken (ed.) 1988, pp. 55–112.

Gatens, Moira and Lloyd, Genevieve, 1999. *Collective Imaginings: Spinoza, Past and Present.* London and New York: Routledge.

Gleick, James, 1988. *Chaos: Making a New Science.* New York: Penguin.

Goodchild, Philip, 1996. *Gilles Deleuze and the Question of Philosophy.* London: Associated University Presses.

Goodwin, Brian, 1984, 'A Relational or Field Theory of Reproduction and its Evolutionary Implications', in Ho and Saunders (eds) 1984, pp. 219–242.

——, 1997. *How the Leopard Changed its Spots.* London: Phoenix.

Goodwin, B., Sibatani, A. and Webster, G. (eds), 1989. *Dynamic Structures in Biology.* Edinburgh: Edinburgh University Press.

Gould, S. J. and Lewontin, R. C., 1979. 'The Spandrels of San Marco and the Panglossian Paradigm: A Critique of the Adaptationist Programme', *Proceedings of the Royal Society of London*, B 205: 581–98.

Grassé, Pierre-Paul, 1977. *Evolution of Living Organisms.* New York: Academic Press.

Grene, Marjorie (ed.), 1973. *Spinoza: A Collection of Critical Essays.* New York: Anchor Books.

Griffen, David R. (ed.), 1986. *Physics and the Ultimate Significance of Time.* Albany, NY: State University of New York Press.

Grosz, Elizabeth, 1994. *Volatile Bodies: Towards a Corporeal Feminism.* London: Allen & Unwin.

Guattari, Felix, 1984. *Molecular Revolution: Psychiatry and Politics*, trans. Rosemary Sheed. Harmondsworth: Penguin.

——, 1995. *Chaosmosis: An Ethico-Aesthetic Paradigm*, trans. Paul Bains and Julian Pefanis. Sydney: Power Publications.

——, 1996. *The Guattari Reader*, ed. Gary Genosko. Oxford: Basil Blackwell.

Gunter, Pete A. Y., 1983. 'Philosophical Method and Biological Time', introduction to the UPA edition of *Creative Evolution*. Lantham, MD: University Press of America.

——, (ed.), 1969. *Bergson and the Evolution of Physics*. Knoxville, TN: University of Tenessee Press.

Hallett, Michael, 1984. *Cantorian Set Theory and the Limitation of Size*. Oxford: Clarendon Press.

Hardt, Michael, 1993. *Gilles Deleuze: An Apprenticeship in Philosophy*. Minneapolis, MN: University of Minnesota Press.

——, and Negri, Antonio, 1994. *Empire*. Cambridge, MA, and London: Harvard University Press.

Hayles, N. Katherine, 1990. *Chaos Bound: Orderly Disorder in Contemporary Literature and Science*. Ithaca, NY: Cornell University Press.

Herken, Rolf (ed.), 1988. *The Universal Turing Machine: A Half-Century Survey*. Oxford: Oxford University Press.

Ho, Mae-Wan, 1984, 'Environment and Heredity in Development and Evolution', in Ho and Saunders (eds) 1984, pp. 267–90.

——, 1989, 'A Structuralism of Process: Towards a Post-Darwinian Rational Morphology', in Goodwin, Sibatani and Webster (eds) 1989, pp. 31–48.

——, 1993. *The Rainbow and the Worm*. Singapore: World Scientific.

——, and Saunders, Peter T., 1979, 'Beyond Neo-Darwinism – An Epigenetic Approach to Evolution', *Journal of Theoretical Biology*, 78: 573–91.

——, (eds), 1984. *Beyond Neo-Darwinism*. London: Academic Press.

——, 1984. 'Pluralism and Convergence in Evolutionary Theory', in Ho and Saunders (eds) 1984, pp. 3–14.

Hodges, Andrew, 1988, 'Alan Turing and the Turing Machine', in Herken (ed.) 1988, pp. 3–15.

——, 1992. *Alan Turing: The Enigma*. London: Vintage.

James, William, 1979. *Some Problems of Philosophy*. Cambridge, MA, and London: Harvard University Press.

Jonas, Hans, 1973. 'Spinoza and the Theory of Organsim', in Marjorie Grene (ed.) 1973, pp. 259–78.

Kampis, George, 1988. 'On Systems and Turing Machines', in *Cybernetics and Systems '88*, ed. R. Trappl. Dordrecht: Kluwer, pp. 85–92.

——, 1991. *Self-Modifying Systems in Biology and Cognitive Science.* Oxford: Pergamon Press.

——, 1993. 'Creative Evolution', *World Futures*, 38: 131–7.

——, and Csányi, V., 1990. 'Coevolution and the Units of Evolution', in J. Maynard Smith and Gary Vida (eds), *Organizational Constraints on the Dynamics of Evolution.* Manchester: Manchester University Press, pp. 385–97.

Kant, Immanuel, 1989. *The Critique of Judgement*, trans. James Meredith. Oxford: Oxford University Press.

——, 1993. *Critique of Pure Reason*, ed. Vasilis Politis. London: J. M. Dent.

Kline, Morris, 1990. *Mathematical Thought from Ancient to Modern Times: Volume 3.* Oxford: Oxford University Press.

Kolakowski, L., 1985. *Bergson.* Oxford: Oxford University Press.

Lacey, A. R., 1989. *Bergson.* London and New York: Routledge.

Leibniz, G. W., 1991. *Monadology*, ed. and anot. Nicholas Rescher. London: Routledge.

Lloyd, Genevieve, 1993. *Being in Time: Selves and Narrators in Philosophy and Literature.* New York and London: Routledge.

——, 1996. *Spinoza and the Ethics.* New York and London: Routledge.

Mandelbrot, Benoit, 1977. *Fractals: Form, Chance and Dimension.* San Francisco, CA: Freeman.

Manheim, Jerome H., 1964. *The Genesis of Point Set Topology.* Oxford: Pergamon Press.

Margulis, Lynn and Sagan, Dorion, 1997. *Microcosmos.* Berkeley, CA: University of California Press.

Marx, Karl, 1993. *Grundrisse*, trans. Martin Nicolaus. London: Penguin.

——, 1998. *The German Ideology: Including* Theses on Feuerbach *and* introduction to The Critique of Political Economy. New York: Prometheus Books.

——, 1999. *Capital: An Abridged Edition*, ed. David McLellan. Oxford: Oxford University Press.

Massumi, Brian, 1992. *A User's Guide to Capitalism and Schizophrenia.* Cambridge and London: MIT Press.

——, 1995. 'The Autonomy of Affect', *Cultural Critique*, 32 (Fall): 85–109.

Moore, A. W., 1990. *The Infinite*. London and New York: Routledge.

Moore, F. C. T., 1996. *Bergson: Thinking Backwards*. Cambridge: Cambridge University Press.

Negri, Antonio, 1991. *The Savage Anomaly*, trans. Michael Hardt. Minneapolis, MN: University of Minnesota Press.

Nietzsche, Friedrich, 1968. *The Will to Power*, ed. Walter Kaufmann, trans. Walter Kaufmann and R. J. Hollingdale. New York: Vintage Books.

———, 1994. *On the Genealogy of Morality*, ed. Keith Ansell Pearson, trans. Carol Diethe. Cambridge: Cambridge University Press.

Papanicolaou, Andrew C. and Gunter, P. A. Y., 1987. *Bergson and Modern Thought*. Chur, Switzerland: Harwood Academic.

Patton, Paul (ed.), 1996. *Deleuze: A Critical Reader*. Oxford: Blackwell.

Penrose, Roger, 1988. 'On the Physics and Mathematics of Thought', in Herken (ed.) 1988, pp. 491–522.

Poincaré, Henri, 1952. *Science and Hypothesis*. New York: Dover Publications.

Post, Emil, 1944. 'Recursively Enumerable Sets of Positive Integers and their Decision Problems', in Davis (ed.) 1965, pp. 304–38.

———, 1965. 'Absolutely Unsolvable Problems and Relatively Undecidable Propositions – Account of an Application', in Davis (ed.) 1965, pp. 338–433.

Prigogine, Ilya, 1980. *From Being to Becoming*. San Francisco, CA: W. H. Freeman.

———, 1988. 'Review of *Bergson and Modern Thought*', ed. A. C. Papanicolaou and Pete A. Y. Gunter, *Texas Books in Review*, 8 (3): 167–81.

———, 1997. *The End of Certainty*. New York: The Free Press.

———, and Stengers, Isabelle, 1985. *Order Out of Chaos*. London: Fontana.

Rotman, Brian, 1993. *Ad Infinitum: The Ghost in Turing's Machine*. Stanford, CA: Stanford University Press.

———, and Kneebone, G. T., 1966. *The Theory of Sets and Transfinite Numbers*. London: Oldbourne.

Ruhe, Algot and Paul, Nancy Margaret, 1914. *Henri Bergson: An Account of his Life and Philosophy*. London: Macmillan.

Russell, Bertrand, 1912. 'The Philosophy of Bergson', in Slater (ed.) 1992, pp. 320–37.

——, 1913. 'Review of *An Introduction to Metaphysics*', in Slater (ed.) 1992, pp. 340–41.

——, 1918. 'The Philosophy of Logical Atomism', in Slater (ed.) 1986, pp. 157–244.

——, 1953. *Mysticism and Logic*. London: Pelican.

——, 1964. *The Principles of Mathematics*. London: Allen & Unwin.

Saunders, Peter T., 1984. 'Development and Evolution', in Ho and Saunders (eds) 1984, pp. 243–63.

——, and Ho, M. W., 1976. 'On the Increase of Complexity in Evolution', *Journal of Theoretical Biology*, 63: 375–84.

——, 1981. 'On the Increase of Complexity in Evolution II. The Relativity of Complexity and the Principle of Minimum Increase', *Journal of Theoretical Biology*, 90: 515–30.

Schrödinger, Erwin, 1996. *Nature and the Greeks* and *Science and Humanism*. Cambridge: Cambridge University Press.

Serres, Michel, 1982. *Hermes: Literature, Science, Philosophy*, ed. Josue V. Harari and David F. Bell. Baltimore, MD: Johns Hopkins University Press.

——, 1991. *Rome: The Book of Foundations*, trans. Felicia McCarren. Stanford, CA: Stanford University Press.

——, with Latour, Bruno, 1995. *Conversations on Science, Culture and Time*, trans. Roxanne Lapidus. Ann Arbor, MI: University of Michigan Press.

Simondon, Gilbert, 1992. 'The Genesis of the Individual', trans. Mark Cohen and Sanford Kwinter, in *Incorporations*. New York: Zone, pp. 297–319.

Slater, John G. (ed.), 1986. *The Collected Papers of Bertrand Russell, Volume 8*. London: Allen & Unwin.

——, 1992. *The Collected Papers of Bertrand Russell, Volume 6*. London and New York: Routledge.

Sontag, Susan (ed.), 1976. *Antonin Artaud: Selected Writings*, trans. Helen Weaver. Berkeley, CA: University of California Press.

Spinoza, Baruch, 1989. *Ethics*, trans. Andrew Boyle, rev. G. H. R. Parkinson. London: J. M. Dent.

Steele, Edward J., Lindley, Robin A. and Blandon, Robert V., 1998. *Lamarck's Signature*. Sydney: Allen & Unwin.

Thom, René, 1972. 'Structuralism and Biology', in C. H. Waddington (ed.) 1972, pp. 68–82.

——, 1989. 'A Formalism Linking Structure With Function', in Goodwin, Sibatani and Webster (eds) 1989, pp. 97–106.

——, 1990. *Semio Physics: A Sketch*, trans. Vendla Meyer. Redwood City, CA: Addison–Wesley.

Thompson, D'Arcy W., 1992. *On Growth and Form*. Cambridge: Cambridge University Press.

Tiles, Mary, 1989. *The Philosophy of Set Theory: An Introduction to Cantor's Paradise*. Oxford and New York: Basil Blackwell.

Turing, Alan, 1936. 'On Computable Numbers, With an Application to the *Entscheidungsproblem*', in Davis (ed.) 1965, pp. 116–51.

——, 1939. 'Systems of Logic Based on Ordinals', in Davis (ed.) 1965, pp. 155–222.

——, 1950. 'Computing Machinery and Intelligence', in Anderson (ed.) 1964, pp. 4–30.

——, 1992. *Collected Works of A. M. Turing: Morphogenesis*, P. T. Saunders. Amsterdam: Elsevier Science.

Virno, Paolo, and Hardt, Michael (eds), 1996. *Radical Thought in Italy*. Minneapolis, MN: University of Minnesota Press.

Waddington, C. H. (ed.), 1972. *Towards a Theoretical Biology: Vol. 4*. Edinburgh: Edinburgh University Press.

Webster, Gerry, 1984. 'The Relations of Natural Forms', in Ho and Saunders (eds), 1984, pp. 193–217.

Whitehead, A. N., 1920. *The Concept of Nature*. Cambridge: Cambridge University Press.

——, 1938. *Science and the Modern World*. London: Penguin.

——, 1978. *Process and Reality: An Essay in Cosmology*, David Ray Griffen and Donald W. Sherburne (eds), New York: The Free Press.

Wildon Carr, H., 1911. *Henri Bergson: The Philosophy of Change*. London: Dodge.

Wood, Alan, 1957. *Bertrand Russell: The Passionate Sceptic*. London: Allen & Unwin.

Zizek, Slavoj, 1999. *The Ticklish Subject*. London and New York: Verso.

Contents